LOOSED FROM THE TASKMASTER

✤

SAM CARR

Contents

1. Three Taskmasters 1

2. How To Recognize the Taskmaster in Your Life 19

3. How To Get Rid of a Taskmaster Mentality 29

4. Eleven Freedom Principles, Part 1 51

5. Eleven Freedom Principles, Part 2 77

Preface

There is no greater time than right now for God's people to awake to righteousness and realize the fact that God has made them free! While drugs, illicit sex, and crime are rampant in our society today, believers can walk free of their pasts in the light of their new life in Christ. They can be *loosed* from the bondages of Satan, sin, and the world, and enjoy liberty, peace, and joy through the power of God.

Satan is a taskmaster, and he wants to browbeat, depress, chasten, and abuse people today, even Christians if they will let him. He wants to cloud and confuse the minds of believers with the darkness of the past so that they never rise to the level of freedom that belongs to them in Christ.

But just because Satan desires to bind you up and keep you bound doesn't mean that he can! Armed with the knowledge of God's Word and the reinforcement of God's power, you can be *loosed* from the taskmaster, and you can *stay* loosed!

It is my prayer that as you read this book — whether you are battling fear, condemnation, drugs, cigarettes, alcohol, sickness, poverty, or *anything* that binds you — you will shed the bondages that have held you back in your walk with God, and learn to walk in the glorious liberty wherewith Christ has made you free!

Chapter 1
Three Taskmasters

Satan is and always has been the enemy of God's people. He is a "taskmaster" who wants to lord it over believers. He wants to oppress them and *keep* them oppressed and bound.

God is and always has been the *Deliverer* of His people. He is still in the business of setting people free today. Jesus paid the price so that people everywhere, from all walks of life, could walk in complete victory.

I believe we can follow biblical principles and learn how to appropriate that victory and experience freedom in life from whatever tries to bind us.

There is certainly no more dramatic an account of deliverance in the Bible than that of the Israelites' deliverance from Egypt under the leadership of Moses. There is no better account than this one that represents Satan's oppression of God's people.

This Old Testament account begins when the children of Israel of Jacob's household were in Egypt after the death of Joseph. The favorite son of Jacob and the one who'd had such great favor with Pharaoh was gone. (If you'll study the Word of God, you will find that Egypt is a type of the world and the world system. Pharaoh is a type of Satan, and the children of Israel are a type of the Church.)

The Bible says that another pharaoh or king was raised up who didn't know Joseph. This new pharaoh didn't understand the covenant relationship that Joseph had had with the previous pharaoh.

EXODUS 1:8-14

8 Now there arose up a new king over Egypt, which knew not Joseph.

9 And he said unto his people, Behold, the people of the children of Israel are more and mightier than we:

10 Come on, let us deal wisely with them; lest they multiply, and it come to pass, that, when there falleth out any war, they join also unto our enemies, and fight against us, and so get them up out of the land.

11 Therefore they did set over them taskmasters to afflict them with their burdens. And they built for Pharaoh treasure cities, Pithom and Raamses.

12 But the more they afflicted them, the more they multiplied and grew. And they were grieved because of the children of Israel.

13 And the Egyptians made the children of Israel to serve with rigour:

14 And they made their lives bitter with hard bondage, in morter, and in brick, and in all manner of service in the field: all their service, wherein they made them serve, was with rigour.

Let me paraphrase what the new pharaoh said in verses 9 and 10. He said, "Listen, if we don't do something about all of these *'Christians'* to keep them bound, they're going to rise up against us, challenge us, and overtake us."

Contrary to popular Christian belief, God did not set the devil over His people to keep them under! The devil is a thief who stole authority from Adam. He comes to steal, kill, and destroy (John 10:10). Pharaoh was a representation of Satan in thought, word, and deed. His thought processes were the same as the devil's. The devil says about us as believers, "We've got to keep these people down!"

So what did the pharaoh do? Verse 11 tells us: *"Therefore they did set over them TASKMASTERS to AFFLICT them with their BURDENS. . . ."*

Look what happened when the children of Israel were afflicted.

EXODUS 1:12
12 But the more they afflicted them, the more they multiplied and grew. And they were grieved because of the children of Israel.

Something interesting about the Christian faith is, the more you as a Christian are persecuted, the stronger you should get.

Most people would probably be quick to agree with me, but many don't have any idea what real persecution is. If you were to walk the streets of some of the Muslim countries and mention the Name of Jesus, you'd find out what persecution is when they started picking up rocks!

Persecution for the Gospel's sake happens every day. Did you know that there are more Christians being martyred today than ever before in the history of the world? There are places where you can be sentenced to death if you witness, and especially if you convert someone.

God's People Are a Threat
To the Devil and the World

I want you to read again what the new pharaoh of Egypt proposed to do to God's people.

EXODUS 1:10
10 Come on, let us deal wisely with them; lest they multiply, and it come to pass, that, when there falleth out any war, they join also unto our enemies, and fight against us, and so get them up out of the land.

Notice how this pharaoh justified the action he proposed. Even today, natural leaders will justify why they want to "cut off" Christians. Their excuses sound justifiable and reasonable to them. They will say something, such as, "After all, we have become a multiethnic, multicultural nation with many diverse religions. It wouldn't be fair for us to give religious preference to Christians, so we're going to have to say we're not giving preference to *any* religion." Not only *could* this happen, I believe it *will* happen.

That's what happened to God's people when Joseph died.

Continue reading in verse 11.

EXODUS 1:11
11 Therefore they did set over them TASKMASTERS to afflict them with their burdens....

We read here that taskmasters were appointed over God's children. The devil tries to do the same thing today. He has appointed taskmasters — demon spirits — over God's children to try to oppress them. The devil wants to press Christians into a mold, so to speak, that will keep them from doing what God wants them to do and from being what He wants them to be. The pharaoh of Egypt was doing to God's people in the Old Testament what the god of this world, Satan (2 Cor. 4:4), tries to do to God's people today.

In Exodus chapter 1, there were three areas in which these taskmasters lorded it over the children of Israel. We're going to look in detail each of these three taskmasters and how they burdened and oppressed God's people.

The First Taskmaster:
The Chief of Tribute

First, there was the *chief of tribute* who controlled the money (*see* Exodus 1:11). "Tribute" was an exorbitant charge levied on the people. Pharaoh and his officials controlled how much money the children of Israel made and how much they kept. Every time it seemed as if the Israelites had a little something, the Egyptians put a tax on them to take that money away from them — to exact it from them. They made sure the Israelites' money was taxed or stolen so that they would never have enough. The Egyptians reasoned that if the children of Israel started gaining wealth, they would also start gaining some power or control.

The devil has sown the lie into the Church that we don't need money. He wants us to think, *We just need Jesus, and everything will be all right.* We often hear a New Testament scripture misquoted: "Money is the root of all evil." No, money is not evil. The Bible says the *love* of money is the root of all evil (1 Tim. 6:10). What a person does with his money can be evil. What a person does *for* money can be evil. However, money in itself is not evil.

God Wants Us To Have Money

Certainly, I agree that we need Jesus. But we need money too. Virtually every believer in God from time immemorial had to have money or some means of bartering or trading in order to live. Even Jesus when He walked on the earth had to have money. For example, how do you think Jesus ate? Also, Jesus' ministry had a treasurer, so we know Jesus had some money.

Additionally, how do you think Joseph, Mary, and Jesus lived in Egypt in the early years when they had to flee Herod? The wise men brought them money.

It takes money to live in this world. And for the Christian, there *is* a way to prosper and have your needs met. You can do it the world's way and ride the "ups and downs" of the world's economic system, and you can even be successful to a degree. However, that does not mean that your prosperity is of God.

God's Way Is Always the Best Way

Another way to prosper is to do it God's way. God has a way to break the yoke of the "chief of tribute" off your life. But as long as you see your job as your only source, then what you make at that job is all you are ever going to have.

Unless you work for a church or ministry, you are probably employed in the secular workplace, which is dominated by the world system. But the moment you make God your source, you can move out of that system, so to speak, and your prosperity can become limitless. You can say, "Father, You are my source. My resources are Your resources. Therefore, *Your* resources are *my* resources."

Then when you begin to release yourself to the Gospel to make your finances available to God, you remove yourself from the world's financial system. You begin to give, looking for ways to bless other people, and the oppression of the chief of tribute begins to be broken in your life! No longer are you bound by receiving only what you earn at your job. You get on *God's* system of prosperity.

The world

Use the World System Wisely

In First Corinthians 7:31, the Apostle Paul was very clear about the world system when he said, "Use the world system, but don't abuse it." Paul used the world system. He worked, but his trade wasn't his source. *God* was Paul's source. We know that, because he said to the Church at Philippi, "...*my God shall supply all your need ACCORDING TO HIS RICHES in glory by Christ Jesus*" (Phil. 4:19).

There's Power in the Choices You Make — Will You Go *God's* Way or the *World's* Way?

You need to realize that the devil wants to control your money. He wants to steal your finances. He wants to keep you on a level where you are just barely making your budget every month, and if something goes wrong, you are in trouble. Well, without your having and acting on the knowledge of God's Word, something *will* go wrong, because the taskmaster wants to bind you up financially. That's why he's called the taskmaster, the "chief of tribute."

Many people reading this book could probably say, "I have a money problem." And the money "problem" for most people is a lack thereof! But I want to tell you something. Our problem is usually not a lack of money. It is not being willing to do things God's way in order to break the yoke of the chief of tribute off of us — to break the power of demonic forces that would try to stop us from rising above what the world says we can have. We have to quit living on the world system and paying exorbitant interest on credit-card debt all our life! We have to decide to stop doing things the world's way and make up our minds to take control of our destinies financially.

The world and the devil think they can control us with money. But when you take what you have and surrender it to God — when you commit yourself and your giving to the Lord — then God will begin to use your money and work through it. When that happens, you will be free.

The Chief of Tribute
Is No Match for God's Word

Every person is different. No two people's experiences are going to be the same. But I can tell you from the standpoint of a pastor and a minister that God's Word works. I am a blessed man today, but I can look back over my life and see several times when I was bound hard and fast by the chief of tribute. I had to make a choice to stay with God's way — or go sell *Amway*! (Many pastors have gone *Am*way instead of *God's* way.)

I'm not saying there is anything wrong with Amway. But I am saying that something is wrong if I use my pulpit or my divine authority as a pastor to sell it! There were times when my wife, Becky, and I looked at our financial situation and had to make a choice. There was a time when we had bill collectors calling us, and, although this happened long ago, it was while we were in the ministry! It wasn't very pleasant. But in the midst of it, we learned what God's Word says about giving and that if we gave, it would be given unto us *". . .good measure, pressed down, and shaken together, and running over, shall men give into your bosom. . ."* (Luke 6:38).

Stay With God's Plan and Be Promoted

I learned that if I stayed with God's plan, I was going to break the yoke of the chief of tribute in my life and be able to move up to another level financially. I'm not talking about just getting more money for *me*. I'm talking about arriving at another level of prosperity that would enable me to do more for the Kingdom of God. Today I'm able to give more than I even earned when I first went in the ministry. Years ago, if Becky hadn't worked as a school teacher, we wouldn't have had enough money to buy food and the basic necessities. Divine prosperity happened for us because we made up our minds that we were not going to stay bound.

There is a direct effort by the enemy to keep the Body of Christ out of the till of the wealth that is on this earth. The chief of tribute wants God's people to be broke! But you can defeat him and get yours — you can get what belongs to you!. No one else may choose to get his, but if you make up your mind to do it God's way, you can get the money that you need and more!

Doing Things God's Way Includes *Giving*

You might ask, "Exactly how do I do it God's way?" By *giving*. You may have heard that time and time again, but you really do need to give. I realize that it can sound self-serving for the pastor of a church to tell his congregation to give, but I know of no other way to help people break the yoke of the chief of tribute than to tell them the truth. If you give in faith, believing, you will be able to look back years from now and say, "I'm so glad that I did what that preacher advised. I'm so glad I obeyed God and stayed with it. I'm so glad I was obedient to support missions and to bring my tithes to the local church and worship God with them — because look at what God has done in my life. I've broken that yoke!"

You can be loosed from the taskmaster in the area of finances. But the way you are going to be loosed is not by what you *have* but by what you *give*. In other words, you will be loosed by how you release or expend what you have — by what you do with your money. As you give in obedience to God and His Word, God will begin to bring liberty to you in the area of finances. The more at liberty you are, the more free you will be to give more, and you will be blessed more and more financially. You will be loosed from the taskmaster and from barely having enough in life.

Don't Let Fear Bind You

Many people who have money are bound to it to the point they are afraid to give any. They say, "Well, I'd better not give. Something might happen, and I might need that money." That is a deception of the enemy to keep them from prospering and increasing even more. The devil wants to keep you from being able to sow money into the Gospel so that you can *continue* to be blessed.

God has blessed my wife and me in so many ways. I am amazed when I think about all the blessings God has given us. Sometimes it's overwhelming. Then I think about what it is going to be like in another five years, because we are on the right track, and we are going to *stay* on that track. We are not going to quit. We are going to continue believing and increasing and doing more for the Kingdom of God. The yoke of the chief of tribute has been broken, and that yoke is going to *stay* broken.

As I said before, my wife and I are walking and living in victory now, but there were times in my life when I had to make up my mind and say, "I'm going to stay with it. I'm going to break that yoke of the chief of tribute. That demon spirit is not going to bind me or my ministry."

The chief of tribute that tries to keep you broke is demonic. And the minute you start making up your mind to believe God financially, it is almost a given that something is going to happen to make your situation appear worse. That "something" is the devil, and that is where most people quit.

God wants you to be free! And when you give consistently as you are supposed to, the taskmaster, the chief of tribute, can't keep you bound financially anymore. He becomes a powerless foe in your life.

A Christian should not be bound in the area of finances. God *wants* to bless you. He *wants* to meet your needs. In fact, He wants to give you abundantly, far over and above all that you can ask, think, or imagine! (Eph. 3:20). But as long as you let the taskmaster beat you over the head, and you say, "Well, this is just the way it is. I work my job and pay my bills and taxes. I am just going to hold out until retirement so I can collect Social Security," then you will not be loosed from the taskmaster. (We should be believing God, not the government, because when our generation gets to retirement age, there might not *be* any Social Security money.)

The Second Taskmaster:
The Chief of Works

The second taskmaster Pharaoh set over the Hebrew children was the *chief of works* (*see* Exodus 1:13). The chief of works kept the Israelites busy. He kept them running. And, later, when they started complaining about it, Pharaoh said, "They're idle and lazy! They have too much time on their hands. Tell the taskmaster not to give them any more straw for making bricks. They will have to find their own straw and make the same number of bricks in the same amount of time!" (Exod. 5:7,8).

I realize there is a wise saying that idle hands are the devil's workshop. However, there are times when you need to get quiet before God — to back off from the day-to-day tasks of life and spend time with Him. It is not good to be constantly busy. In fact, if all you are doing is working from daylight to dusk with your "nose to the grindstone," without ever looking up or taking a break, then you are bound by the taskmaster.

"Works" means *energy expended*. It *does not* mean *things accomplished.* Did you know you can be so busy working that you do not have time for the things of God? You can fall into the bed at night so tired that you don't have time to read your Bible or pray, and you are too exhausted to get up early.

Some people will say, "I just don't have time to go to church. I'm too busy working." Well, if they don't have time to put God first, they are *too busy!*

A person can even get too busy working in the ministry. In my own life, I have gone to my study in times past to sit down and study, when, suddenly, I'm thinking of ten thousand things I need to do! Do you know who was telling me to do all those things? It was the taskmaster. He says, "Go, go, go! You've got to work, work, work! You can't sit here anymore. You are wasting time. You have places to go, people to see!"

That is not God; it is the taskmaster. And if that scenario describes you, you need to be loosed.

Don't Let Distractions Rob You of God's Blessings

The only way we are going to get into the glory of God is to make up our minds that we are going to wait before Him. We're not going to be in a hurry. We're not going to rush our time alone with God or our time of praise and worship in church. We're not going to say, "Let's hurry up and worship God so we can go home!"

That is what the taskmaster wants you to say. As I said, he wants you to think you are too busy to even go to church. If you yield to him, the taskmaster will keep you so busy that you won't have time for what God really wants for your life. You will spend your life doing things that God never told you to do.

Some people want you to hurry through a church service. If you were to ask them, "Why are you in such a hurry?" they would say, "Well, I want to go watch something on TV. I've got to be home by one o'clock."

That sounds ridiculous, but the devil will try anything to keep you too busy for God. I have heard "busy" people say, "Well, I'm just trying to make a living for my family." But, no, they are not, because making a living for your family includes being *there with* your family where you are all living and fellowship and having a life together. Some ultra-busy people may be providing *money* for their family, but that is not the same as providing a *living* for them.

So don't say, "I'm doing it for my family." You may think you are working hard for them, but you're probably not. You're probably doing it because *you want to work*! Your family may reap the financial benefits of all your work, but it is very possible that you are working for *you*, not for your family.

Put God First and Reap
The Rewards of Faithfulness

The things of God are more important than your work. I realize that there are those who sometimes have to work on Sundays. I am not trying to put those people under condemnation. But I am trying to get people to examine their lives and to put God first. You know, you could be sitting in church, worshipping God, and the Holy Ghost could fall on you and give you one idea that could make you more money than you ever *thought* about making on your job. I have seen it happen. I can show you people in my church whose businesses and lives were totally changed because they first committed themselves to God. When they committed themselves to God, He began to show them what to do. And it did not take away from their time with Him.

The taskmaster, the chief of works, will try to keep you working constantly. He will keep you hopping if he can, and it doesn't have to be anything important that he has you doing — as long as you are too busy for God. He will try to make you too tired, depressed, and worn out to do much of anything.

The Third Taskmaster:
The Chief of Burdens

The third taskmaster Satan will try to oppress you with is called the *chief of burdens* (*see* Exodus 1:14). What is weighing you down? More than likely, if you were to tell me, "Pastor Carr, such-and-such is weighing me down," and I said, "Let's go back five years," we would discover that the things weighing you down today are some of the same things that have weighed you down consistently for many years.

The devil does not know any new tricks. He does the same thing over and over again. And he will do the same thing in *your* life over and over again if you let him. You will have the same burdens, the same weights, and the same things to deal with over and over again until you make up your mind and say, "Enough is enough! I have a right to be free of this, and I *am* free in Jesus' Name!"

The word "burden" means *something carried; something oppressive, worrisome, or cumbersome.* The writer of Hebrews said, "Let us lay aside every weight" (Heb. 12:1). The word "weight" there means *encumbrance.*

Why Worry?

You can get entangled in webs of worry and problems that you don't have any business being involved with. For example, people worry about the economy as if they could do something about it. But what do they think they can really do? Go to Washington D. C., walk up to Mr. Greenspan, and tell him what they think about raising interest rates? They are not going to do that. So why do they worry about it? I'll tell you why. Because the chief of burdens wants them to be burdened.

Release All of Your Burdens to God

I could probably list ten thousand things that could potentially oppress and weigh you down in life. If you let them burden you, they will stop you from moving higher. They will stop you from reaching the heights God wants you to reach and from moving further toward the place God wants you to be in Him. So you are going to have to make up your mind to release the weights and burdens that the taskmaster wants you to carry. Release them and let them go. It is not going to help you to carry those burdens; it is only going to hinder you. Most of the time, it is impossible for you to do anything about them, anyway. But God can. So release them and give them to Him.

As you begin to react to weights, burdens, and sin according to God's Word instead of reacting the way the world tells you to, a wonderful thing will happen. All of a sudden, you will begin to realize, "Something is happening here. I am getting free of these burdens! I am not weighed down as I used to be! I can shout to God and rejoice!"

Jesus Has Set You Free!

Someone might say, "I would release my burdens to God, but you don't understand my situation."

No, I don't, but I do understand that the taskmaster has you bound.

You may have difficult situations in your life. I am in no way making light of that fact. But they do not have to be a *burden*. You can be free. Jesus has set you free! So get yourself in the Word of God, go into your "prayer closet," and begin to seek Him. God will show you the answer. He will lift those burdens off of you, and you will walk free of them.

It starts with your making up your mind to be free, because you *are* free. The taskmaster wants to bind you to your burdens until you are completely weighed down by them. As I said, sometimes it is the same burdens over and over again. Somewhere down the road of life, you are going to have to cut those burdens off. You have to tell the taskmaster, "You have no authority over me. I will not bow to you. I will not respond to you or your burdens any longer, in Jesus' Name!"

The Taskmaster Brings Sorrow — Jesus Brings Joy

Now God eventually delivered the children of Israel from Egypt — from Pharaoh and the taskmasters. Exodus 3:7 gives a description of the mercy and compassion of God and His willingness to deliver His people from the oppression of the taskmaster.

> **EXODUS 3:7**
> 7 And the Lord said, I have surely seen the affliction of my people which are in Egypt, and have heard their cry BY REASON OF THEIR TASKMASTERS; for I know their sorrows.

Here is the good news. If you are bound up and you cry out to God, He will hear you by reason of your taskmasters — by reason of your trouble. If you do not have enough money or if you are bound in the area of works or burdens, God will hear you by reason of your difficulty. He will hear your cry and will work in your behalf.

By reason of their taskmasters. That is a powerful phrase. God is just waiting for you to cry out to Him, *"Help!"* He is waiting for you to say, "Father, I am going to believe You, stand my ground, and *expect* You to move. I am not going to worry about this.

The Devil is a cruel taskmaster.
God is a master of tasks.

I'm going to cast the care of it over on You [1 Peter 5:7]. I thank You that Your peace is mine that passes all understanding, and it mounts a guard over my heart and mind [Phil. 4:7]. I will not have a care in the world over this."

God Hears Your Cry

God said He was willing to move in the lives of the children of Israel because of the taskmasters. And He was willing to do it because of what He heard: *". . .I [the Lord] have surely seen the affliction of my people which are in Egypt, and have HEARD THEIR CRY by reason of their taskmasters. . ."* (Exod. 3:7).

I looked up the word "cry," and it can also mean *sigh* and *groan.* God heard the sighs and groanings of His people. I hear people today crying out, "Oh, if only I had more money," "If only I could receive healing for my body," "If only I had more time," or "If only I didn't have this or that to worry about." But God hears the cries of His people today, just as He heard the Israelites' cries back then.

Now look at Exodus 3:8.

EXODUS 3:8
8 And I am come down to deliver them out of the hand of the Egyptians, and to bring them up out of that land unto a good land and a large, unto a land flowing with milk and honey. . . .

In other words, God was saying, "Not only will I deliver you from the hands of the taskmaster, but I'm going to bless you. I'm going to meet your needs. I am going to provide the money you need. I am going to give you the energy you need to work for Me. I am going to take care of all those burdens that have weighed you down, and I am going to put you in a place of peace, a place of joy, a place of glory."

No taskmaster in the world can keep you bound when you decide to be free.

Chapter 2
How To Recognize the Taskmaster in Your Life

In Chapter 1, I talked about three taskmasters from Exodus 1 — the *chief of tribute*, the *chief of works*, and the *chief of burdens* — and how they dominated and oppressed God's people, the children of Israel. I also compared these taskmasters to the devil and his cohorts who want to rule over God's people today.

You might say, "Pastor Carr, all that sounds interesting, but we don't have taskmasters today."

Certainly, we do. Just look around you. Do you see Christians who are bound? Paul called the taskmaster "a messenger of Satan sent to buffet him" (2 Cor. 12:7). Of course, Paul did not let the devil control him, but the devil was a thorn in Paul's flesh, so to speak, that buffeted him.

All the things that happen to you are not just happenstance. Many of the things that happen to you are due to the fact that there is a messenger of Satan who is trying to buffet you — trying to cause you to pay tribute to the world and to give money to the world that should go to God. Do not kid yourself into thinking that the devil does not try to do that. He does, and do you know his number one way of doing that? It is called *interest!*

To oppress you financially is the job of the chief of tribute.

We also talked about a taskmaster called the chief of *works.* The devil is very skilled at getting you so involved in *works* that you do not get involved with *God.* He knows how to keep you so busy that you cannot hear from God or take time for God and the things of God.

The devil has tried to appoint taskmasters over God's people, but, personally, I do not work for him! I do not *have* to put up with him, and I do not *intend* to put up with him.

The Lust of the Flesh, the Lust of the Eye,
And the Pride of Life

I do not want you to get the idea that all of our problems in life come from the devil. They do not. In fact, the Bible teaches that we are drawn away by our own lusts (James 1:14) — by the *lust of the flesh*, the *lust of the eye*, and the *pride of life*.

"What is that?" you might ask. The *lust of the flesh* is simple. It says, "I want to." There is no other reason than "I want to."

The *lust of the eye* says, "I want to, and I have a reason. I *see* it."

The *pride of life* says, "I want to. I see it, and I have a another reason. I can handle it." When you get yourself into any one of those places, you have submitted to the taskmaster.

What does a taskmaster do? We went over some of it from Exodus 1. You need to recognize the areas of your life where the taskmaster has perhaps had some influence over you.

The Taskmaster Will Try To *Browbeat* You

The job of the taskmaster is to *afflict*. There are four ways in which he afflicts, based on different meanings of the word "afflict." The *first* way he afflicts is to *browbeat*. The word "browbeat" means *to depress or abash with arrogant speech*.

Did you know that the world is arrogant? You could meet someone unsaved who is just as meek and mild-mannered as he can be, but the minute you start talking about Jesus, all of a sudden, that arrogance and indignation rise up!

The world will "look down their nose" at you when you start talking about Jesus. There is an arrogance that arises in them. I have been amazed at times, talking to different unsaved people who I thought were just as sweet as they could be. Then I start talking to one of them about Jesus, and the next minute, I am asking myself, *Who is this person? He's not who I thought he was!*

Do you know people who always seem to want to beat you down with their words? How many people have you run across who "talk down" to you because you are a Christian — because you serve God and you are walking in the flow of His Spirit? They talk to you as if you are on a lower level than they are — as if you are low-down, no good, and pitiful. They say things, such as, "You just need Christianity for an emotional crutch in your life."

Thank God, that "emotional crutch" keeps *me* healthy! It keeps my family healthy, and it keeps us together. It keeps me on the right track in life and keeps my needs met! I use that "crutch" constantly. Thank God for it. Give me another one!

The taskmaster *afflicts.* He will try to browbeat you every chance he gets. He will try to lord it over you by using arrogant speech to try to dominate you. You have to ask the question, "Am I going to stay with the things of God — or am I going to let the taskmaster browbeat me and keep me down?"

The Taskmaster Will Try To Make
You *Depressed*

One of the first things you have to do to walk free from the taskmaster is to recognize his devices. The Bible says, *"Lest Satan should get an advantage of us: for we are not ignorant of his devices"* (2 Cor. 2:11). We know that Satan, the taskmaster, has been assigned to try to afflict us. And we know that one of the ways he does that is to try to *browbeat* us. Another way he does it is to try to *depress* us.

So a *second* definition of the word "afflict" is to *depress*. The word "depress" means *failure to withstand or bear up under weight and stresses, the resulting state being lowered activity, dullness, or dejection.*

That means that if the devil can beat you down enough over your problem — over your being bound up — he will make you depressed. You will start moving in slow motion, so to speak. You will not want to do anything. You will not be active. You will be dull. And you certainly will not accomplish anything for the Kingdom of God. That is right where the devil wants you — in a lowered state of activity. He wants you a little dull and dejected. He wants you in a position where you do not go too high or too far in the things of God.

A young man came to me awhile back who was involved in a denominational ministry, and he had been watching our ministry program, "Here's Life," on television. He began getting hungry for more of God and His Word and said, "I know there's more. There has to be more to the Christian life."

This young man first went for encouragement to one of his family members who was a minister in the same denomination. The young man said, "I'm losing my zeal for God. I don't *want* to lose my zeal, but I am. There's got to be more."

This family member just gave the young man a pat on the back and said, "That's all right, Son. We all lose our zeal after a while."

That is exactly what the devil wants you to believe. That is exactly where he wants you — in a place where you are not doing what you should be doing.

That young man who had seen our broadcast ended up getting filled with the Holy Ghost and experiencing the fullness of God — at which time he promptly got the "left foot of fellowship" from his denomination!

The Taskmaster Will Try To *Chasten* You

A third way the taskmaster afflicts is to *chasten*. "Chasten" in the context of affliction means *to correct by punishment or suffering*. We have been so confused about what God does and what the devil does that we think God is the one who is abusing the Body of Christ! But it is not God; it is the devil! Someone who is being afflicted might say, "God is trying to teach me something." No, the *devil* is trying to knock him down so he will learn not to get back up! The devil, not God, is the taskmaster.

The Taskmaster Will Try To *Abuse* You

A *fourth* definition of "afflict" is to *abuse*. The word "abuse" means *to be harsh or unfair*.

If you are a Christian and you talk about God, Jesus, and the power of the Holy Ghost, people are going to talk about you.

They are going to talk behind your back, and they are going to talk to your face! You might as well get ready for it. The taskmaster is going to see that it happens. One way or another, he will try to beat you up one side and down the other! I am not trying to glorify that fact. I am just *telling* you that fact! (However, just because the taskmaster wants to beat you down and keep you there does not mean it has to be that way.)

No one ever said that you would be treated fairly as a Christian. We have perhaps gotten the idea that we would be because we have lived with "Joseph" — we have enjoyed a certain degree of favor. Let me tell you something. "Joseph" has died, and our favor with the world is diminishing. The world will try to abuse us. They will speak harshly against us. In the past, they would not dare say anything, but they do now. It is not going to get any better; it is going to get worse.

All of these things happened to the children of Israel. They were *browbeaten, depressed, chastened,* and *abused* by their taskmasters. Not only does the Bible say that Pharaoh set taskmasters over them and afflicted them with burdens, but it also goes on to say that the Egyptians made the children of Israel to serve with *rigor* (Exod. 1:11,13). That word "rigor" means *to break apart* or *to break down.*

The devil wants to break you down. He wants to push you and push you until you break down and become just a Sunday morning Christian on your way to Heaven. You see, that is what the Egyptians were afraid of — they were afraid of the Israelites' zeal for God. They were afraid the

Israelites would rise up and become a mighty army. So they afflicted them with taskmasters to try to hold them down.

Here is the good news — God's people were delivered! Moses led them out of Egypt. Moses led them out of the "world" the same way that Jesus led *us* out of the "world" — away from the taskmaster!

Our Contention Is Spiritual, Not Natural

Ephesians 6:12 very plainly tells us that we as Christians ". . .*wrestle* [contend] *not against flesh and blood, but against principalities, against powers, against the rulers of the darkness of this world, against spiritual wickedness in high places."* The Greek translates "spiritual wickedness" in this verse as *wicked spirits.*

If you think that as a Christian you are going to get along with the world, you are sadly mistaken. There is a contention there. It is not a social contention, such as the kind that occurs when people carry signs outside an abortion clinic, for example. People who do that believe they are fighting the devil, but they are not. They are dealing with a social issue using natural means. I am not saying that is necessarily wrong, but it is not spiritual warfare or contention that they are involved in. The Apostle Paul traveled to Athens, one of the most ungodly places on the face of the earth during the time of his missionary journeys. The people of Athens offered babies for sacrifices to their gods!

What did Paul do? He didn't walk around with a big placard that said, "Jesus lives!" or "Jesus loves you." No, Paul just got up before the people and started preaching the Gospel!

He did the same thing in Ephesus, and some people became angry while others became glad. That is the way the Gospel works. Some people get glad and some get mad. You will never get everyone to be glad. Everyone is not going to be happy about the Gospel or the Good News. So what do you do? You just preach or witness to the next person. God is preparing people's hearts. He knows who will receive.

The 'Imprint' of the World

As Christians, we are in the world, but we are not *of* the world (John 17:14). The Bible also says that to be a friend of the world is to be an enemy of God (James 4:4). The Spirit of God has shown me why so many Christians are bound and defeated in life, and I have observed it many, many times myself. A person could be born again and walking in his liberty in Christ, but then he allows the "imprint" of the world to drag him back down. The imprint of the world affects his receiving needed finances, healing for his body, and deliverance from tests and trials. How? He allows circumstances and his physical senses — what he can see, hear, smell, taste, and touch — to be more powerful in his life than what God has said in His Word.

For example, you may go to a church service where you rejoice and praise God and get all excited about the things of God. Then you leave the service and get a phone call from someone who gives you some bad news, and you are right back in the pit God delivered you from in the service. Why? Because you allowed what happened in the world to dictate to you how you were going to live and act — what condition you were going to be in spiritually, emotionally, and physically.

Be Molded By God,
Not the Enemy or the World

There are spiritual forces — taskmasters — in the world that will try to push and mold you in order to make you ineffective in the Kingdom of God. They will try to keep you down. They will try to push you around. They will try to hold you in your little box, in your little world, to keep you from breaking out and moving into greater places and greater heights spiritually. *However, try as they might, those taskmasters cannot defeat you if you will not allow them to!*

Contend for the Faith
And Possess Your Victory!

If the devil could have done it, he would have kept my church at the hotel where we first started holding services, but we contended for the faith. We fought the good fight of faith (1 Tim. 6:12). We stood our ground and believed God. When all "hell" broke loose, we just weathered the storm and kept right on going until we came out on the other side victorious!

The devil would also have loved to have kept us in the little building that is now behind our church, which we now use for a choir room. (We used to hold services there when we left the hotel.) He could not do it.

As long as you contend for the faith, stand your ground, and apply the principles of God's Word without backing off or giving up, sooner or later, you are going to overcome.

The devil wanted us to say, "We're just a small church on the corner. I guess that's all God meant for us to be. Our outreach is just to a few people. And this is all we're ever going to be."

We could have just acquiesced to our circumstances. That is easy to do, but if you bow to circumstances, you will not grow spiritually. More than likely, you will go backward, and you will not realize all that God wants for your life.

We also could have given up after the first time we added on to our current building. We could have said, "We're satisfied. We have a nice facility with wonderful people," and that would have been the extent of our growth. We could have just said, "We're just going to relax and enjoy our success."

However, we made up our minds that, with God's help, we were going to do whatever it took to keep growing. When we did, the devil and demons could not stop us.

Chapter 3
How To Get Rid of
A Taskmaster Mentality

The Bible says that when the children of Israel came out of Egypt, they were free from their taskmasters. How do I know that? Because they had the Egyptians' silver and gold (Exod. 12:36)! The Israelites did not have a care in the world. God gave them a cloud by day and a pillar of fire by night to guide them (Exod. 13:21,22). The sandals on their feet did not wear out (Deut. 29:5), and all they had to do for breakfast was to go outside and gather fresh manna that had come down from Heaven (Exod. 16:15). God totally delivered them.

That is what happened to you when you became saved. God totally delivered you, and you were made free. However, just because you are saved does not mean you don't have a taskmaster *mentality*. A taskmaster mentality will hold you in bondage even though you are really free. As long as you have a taskmaster mentality, the devil will be able to keep you bound.

Using the example of the Israelites, let me show you why many Christians do not walk in their freedom and experience the victory that has already been given to them.

After the children of Israel left Egypt, they were free from their taskmasters, but they still had a taskmaster mentality. When they came to the banks of the Jordan River, where just on the other side was the land flowing with milk and honey that God had promised them, they balked! They were out of Egypt, but *Egypt* was still in *them*.

Just on the other side of that river were all the blessings, benefits, and provisions that God had said belonged to them. The Israelites sent twelve spies into the land, and ten of the twelve came back with an "evil report" of unbelief based on their taskmaster mentality. They said, "Dear God, we can't go in there to possess it. Those people remind us of the Egyptians. They're big and mean, and they've got big, walled cities besides! No way can we do this!" (*see* Numbers 13:31-33).

God delivered the children of Israel out of Egypt, but they never forgot the way they were treated by Pharaoh and the Egyptians. It was still a big part of their thinking. Although God was doing miracles among them in the wilderness, they did not break free from the taskmaster mentality. God was a mighty God to them, providing for them at every turn. Yet they still had indelibly printed on their minds, on their psyches, the fact that they had been bound under taskmasters. So when the time came for them to go into the Promised Land, they faltered.

The children of Israel had been beaten down for so long that they did not think they could do what God Himself had told them they could do. Many in the Body of Christ are like that today.

The Israelites said, in effect, "Poor, pitiful us. All we have is God. We don't have the great armies of Pharaoh." No, they did *not* have the great armies of Pharaoh, *because those armies drowned in the sea when God divided it and caused His people to pass over!*

God had wrought a tremendous victory in the Israelites' lives, but they had forgotten about it. They still had the mentality, "We can't do anything; all we can do is make bricks." That attitude robbed them and literally stopped them from entering into the Promised Land. They did not enter into what God had for them although they were free people. Why? Because they kept thinking they were bound. They had a taskmaster mentality.

The world's taskmasters are hard, but when the world's taskmasters get hold of a believer — one of God's people — it is *twice* as hard. In other words, many Christians today will say the same thing, in essence, that the ten spies said. They will say, "Oh, yes, I know God's promises are true. I know God wants to bless, save, heal, deliver, and prosper people. I know that He wants to deliver me from all bondage. I know He wants me to have a sound mind and to have His wisdom and guidance. I know it's all true, *but I cannot receive it*"!

What the Israelite spies said was, "It's all true, but we've got a problem: The circumstances that we perceive to exist in that land are greater than our perception of God and our ability to overcome them."

Where did that attitude come from? It came from their taskmaster mentality — from the thoughts they still had that they were browbeaten, depressed, chastened, and abused.

The children of Israel saw themselves the same way those taskmasters told them they were. The Egyptian taskmasters had said, "You're lowdown. You're no good.

You're a worthless bunch of renegades. You can't do anything right. You can't do this. You can't do that."

Those taskmasters were constantly badgering, afflicting, beating down, tearing down, and breaking down the children of Israel. When the Israelites arrived at the Promised Land and had the opportunity to enter into God's blessings, all of that rose back up, and they said, "Dear God, we're not big enough in our own sight. We don't have enough confidence in our own ability to do anything. How in the world are we going to take this land?"

Indecision and a Taskmaster Mentality Will Keep You in the Wilderness

Christians do the same thing today. They hear about the blessings of God. They know about them and get excited about them. They look across the "Jordan" at those blessings and say, "Yes, the blessings are for us today!" They go to church because the pastor makes them feel good. He tells them God can do something for them. However, that is as far as many believers go.

At some point, they are going to have to make the decision themselves to step across Jordan and enter their promised land. At some point, they are going to have to say, "Not only are the blessings for us today; they are for *me* today, and I receive them by faith. I am going to face this taskmaster who has stolen my money and has put me under burdens. He has afflicted me and beaten me down. He has challenged me, and I am going to challenge *him*. I am going to stand against him and overcome! I will not be bound any longer!"

If you do not make this important decision, even though you are a Christian, you will spend your life in the wilderness, just as the Israelites did.

Don't Live in the 'Wilderness' Of Compromise and Complacency

Now wilderness life is not too bad. Really, it's not! Read about what happened to the children of Israel in the wilderness. Certainly, I realize they got into rebellion a few times and had some problems, but God did some great things in the wilderness. He fed everyone lunch with quail and toast — manna from Heaven! Bitter waters were made sweet. God even gave them water out of a rock! They experienced all kinds of miracles.

That is where many Christians live. They live in that barren place from day to day. Then when some real crisis comes up, they cry out to God for a miracle, and He always answers. However, they never are able to step across that line where they are no longer bound by the taskmaster. They never are able to *live* in God's rich abundance for them. They are always on the other side of the Jordan, so to speak. They never enter into the full provision.

I do not want to live like that. Do you? I do not want to be bound by the taskmaster in *any* area of my life. I do not like being browbeaten, depressed, chastened, and abused. Certainly, I can get *myself* into trouble at times, and I understand that I am the one, not the devil, who does it. However, just because I get myself into trouble, I am not going to be a slave to it. I have made up my mind, I am not going to be a slave. I am going to do what it takes to receive from God. I am going to find out what the Word says and do it so I can be free!

You have to get rid of a taskmaster mentality. You have to quit letting the devil beat you over the head, keeping you bound because of some problem. You do not have to be bound. You can run to God and get free right in the midst of what you think your worst bondage is. You can be free and become a person of liberty.

Do Not Look Back —
Walk in Your Liberty Today!

If you are bound, it does not matter how *long* you have been bound. It does not matter how entrenched in your thinking that taskmaster mentality is. If you are a child of God, it does not have to be that way. You may have resigned yourself to being bound, saying, "This is just my lot in life." You need to wake up and realize that not only are you a child of God, but you are a joint-heir with Jesus (Rom. 8:17). You are sealed with the Holy Spirit of promise. You have all God has to give — and He has given it! He has given you His Son and His Spirit!

God Wants To Move You
To a Better Place of Grace!

We know that God was saying to the children of Israel when He led them out of Egypt, "Not only will I deliver you from the hands of the taskmaster, but I'm going to *bless* you." God not only desires to set us free, He wants to bless us and bring us into a greater place. He does not just say, "Well, okay, I'm going to set you free from that." No, He also says, "Let Me bring you into a better, greater place."

God always wants to move us up to a greater place and a higher level. It is not a race to see who can get to the highest level. God moves every person along his own particular path in life. Whatever the challenges are that you are overcoming, that is how God is moving you. So do not ever compare yourself to someone else. Just move right along *your* path! Do not get mad if God is doing something for someone else. Just rejoice with him or her and watch God move you along your own path. He wants to move you to a greater place of grace and glory!

Jehovah, Our Deliverer

I want to show you a key that will help you move to greater places and greater heights in God.

EXODUS 6:1,2
1 Then the Lord said unto Moses, Now shalt thou see what I will do to Pharaoh: for with a strong hand shall he let them go, and with a strong hand shall he drive them out of his land.
2 And God spake unto Moses, and said unto him, I AM the Lord.

God told Moses in verse 2, "I am the Lord." That sounds pretty strong, but that is not all He was saying. He was saying, "I am Jehovah" or "I am the Self-Existing One who reveals Himself." So God was saying, in essence, "I am going to be the One who reveals Myself to you." Anytime God wanted to reveal to the children of Israel an aspect of who He really was, He always used the Name "Jehovah" to do it.

God is the God of peace. So He said, "I am Jehovah *Shalom*" (Judges 6:24; John 14:27). He also revealed Himself as the God of righteousness when He said, "I am Jehovah *Tsidqenuw*" (Jer. 23:6; 2 Cor. 5:21). He pronounced Himself as the God who heals when He said, "I am Jehovah *Rapha*" (Exod. 15:26). He revealed Himself as the God who provides when He introduced Himself as Jehovah *Jireh* (Gen. 22:8,14). In other words, God was saying to His people, "I will reveal Myself to you to meet *every need of your life*! *I am* Jehovah."

I am personally a witness to His peace. I am a witness to His righteousness. I am a witness to His healing power. I am a witness to His provision! He has revealed Himself to me and has met my every need!

God was saying to the children of Israel, "I am revealing to you the Name that will bring you out of bondage. I am going to bring you out of bondage. I am going to do it because I am Jehovah."

Jesus, the Fullness of Jehovah

As you study this out, you will find that "Jehovah" is the redemptive Name of God. Anything that Jesus did in God's great plan of redemption, God called Himself that in the Old Testament. The fulfillment of who Jehovah is was revealed in Jesus. Why? Because Jesus is our peace. He is our righteousness. He is our healer. He is our provider. We are complete in Him. Every need is supplied through Jesus Christ. He was and is the fullness of Jehovah.

God was showing the Israelites, "I am going to be Jehovah to you. I am going to be your peace. I am going to be your righteousness. I am going to be your healer. I am going to be your righteousness. I am going to be your provider, your protector, your deliverer. I am the One."

When we really get hold of this, we will fully understand why Jesus said in Luke 13:16, ". . .*ought not this woman, being a daughter of Abraham, whom Satan hath bound, lo, these eighteen years, be loosed from this bond on the sabbath day?*" She had a right to it, because Jehovah God is the deliverer!

Let's continue reading in Exodus chapter 6.

EXODUS 6:3-5
3 And I appeared unto Abraham, unto Isaac, and unto Jacob, by the name of God Almighty, but by my name Jehovah was I not known to them.
4 And I have also established my covenant with them, to give them the land of Canaan, the land of their pilgrimage, wherein they were strangers.
5 And I have also heard the groaning of the children of Israel, whom the Egyptians keep in bondage; and I have remembered my covenant.

Pay close attention to verse 5: "*. . .I have also heard the groaning of the children of Israel, whom the Egyptians keep in bondage; and I HAVE REMEMBERED MY COVENANT.*"

Jehovah heard the groaning of the children of Israel and remembered His covenant. So can you see how this moved Jesus to say to that daughter of Abraham, "Ought not this woman be loosed?" She had a covenant with God, and that is why He says to *you* as a covenant child of God, "Ought not you be loosed?"

We have a right to be free from the taskmaster. We have a right to be free from the chief of tribute. We have a right to be free from the chief of works and from the chief of burdens. We do not have to be bowed down. We can be loosed because of Jehovah God, who sent His Son Jesus to fulfill everything that He had promised to Abraham and made a covenant with him about.

All you and I have to do is make up our mind that we are going to stand our ground and refuse to let the devil steal from us. We are going to stand until we see the answer — until we see our need met.

You Must Endure With Patience the 'Gets-Worse-Before-It-Gets-Better' Syndrome!

Have you ever felt as if you were genuinely believing God, but things seemed only to get worse in your life? You knew Jesus as your Redeemer. You knew you "ought to be loosed," but nothing seemed to be happening.

Moses expressed that same feeling.

EXODUS 5:22,23
22 And Moses returned unto the Lord, and said, Lord, wherefore hast thou so evil entreated this people? why is it that thou hast send me?
23 For since I came to Pharaoh to speak in thy name, he hath done evil to this people; neither hast thou delivered thy people at all.

Have you ever felt like Moses felt? Have you ever said, "Lord, Reverend So-and-so said You were going to loose me! The Bible says You're supposed to supply my needs. However, ever since I heard that message, all I've had is hell! The washing machine broke. The dog bit the postman. The kids broke out a window. I mean, I thought I was going to get my needs met, and now I have even *more* needs!"

Have you ever felt that way? Certainly, you have! Do you

know why? Because, often, a situation gets worse before it gets better. For example, when God first spoke to Moses about delivering His people, and Moses marched in to Pharaoh, it was not exactly the next day when the children of Israel left town! No, in fact, they endured some more afflictions, difficulties, and problems. Yet there came a day when they packed their bags and walked out of that place. No one was sick. Do you know why no one was sick? Because the night before, they had partaken of the Passover lamb. God was remembering His covenant.

Not only was everyone well when they left Egypt, but all who put the blood of the Passover lamb on their door posts the previous night were spared when the angel of death traveled through Egypt in accordance with the word of the Lord (Exod. 12:1-13). Then not only *that*, but the Israelites walked out of captivity with the silver and gold of all the Egyptians. Think about that! That was a type of us leaving the world — not leaving for Heaven — but moving out of the world system.

When you move out of "Egypt," you do not go out barefoot and beaten down. You do not go out poor, sick, and defeated. You go out in victory! Whatever it is you are dealing with, whatever battle you are facing, or whatever your struggle is, you need to make up your mind and proclaim, "Bless God, the chief of tribute, the chief of works, and the chief of burdens are not going to have me. The taskmaster is not going to control me. I am *loosed* because I am a child of Almighty God and a joint-heir with Jesus Christ. I'm in covenant with God, and I am not going to be bound!"

It may look as if things are getting worse before they get better, but, eventually, you are going to walk out of Egypt! You are going to walk out in victory. The world might try to chase you down and tell you, "You can't do that. You're not supposed to do that!" Just keep on going, because those voices will begin to fade away until they are "drowned in the waters" (*see* Exodus 14:28).

Where Do You Draw the Line?

In life, you are the one who chooses at what point you break the yoke of the taskmaster. You have to ask yourself, *Where is that line over which I refuse to go any further without being free?*

Where do *you* draw the line? You are the one who has to ask the question and decide, "Ought not I be loosed, seeing that I am a joint-heir with Jesus Christ and blessed with faithful Abraham?"

> **GALATIANS 3:9,14**
> **9 So then they which be of faith are blessed with faithful Abraham. . . .**
> **14 That the blessing of Abraham might come on the Gentiles through Jesus Christ; that we might receive the promise of the Spirit through faith.**

The Bible also says in Galatians chapter 3:29: *"And if ye be Christ's, then are ye Abraham's seed, and heirs according to the promise."* Always remember that it was because of Abraham that God delivered the children of Israel out of Egypt. God said, "I am going to reveal Myself by a new Name, Jehovah, and I will remember My covenant." He was talking about the covenant He made with Abraham and his descendants (Exod. 6:2,5).

Today, we as believers have a new Name by which God has revealed Himself — *Jesus!* In that Name is all the fullness of the Godhead. You name it, it is in the Name — peace, righteousness, healing, provision, prosperity, protection, and deliverance. It belongs to you and me! Jesus said, *". . .I am come that they might have life, and that they might have it more abundantly"* (John 10:10).

It is time that you as a Christian, a child of God, make up your mind that you have had enough of the taskmasters that have been controlling your life. It does not matter if it is sickness, fear, addiction, lack of finances, or dire poverty — you can be free.

Did you know that there is really no lack of finances in this world? There is plenty of money here. You might not have it in your hand, but it is here. Religion does not want you talking about money, because the taskmaster controls religion.

"How do you know that, Pastor Carr?" It's easy. I know that the taskmaster controls religion, because religion does not want you to have any money, and most religious people are burdened down themselves. All they know to do to get money is to work, work, work.

You see, it does not matter how the devil has tried to mold or push you into religion, tradition, or the world system, you can be loosed from the taskmaster! Even if things get worse before they get better, victory is yours; it belongs to you as a child of God and an heir of Abraham.

Taskmasters From the Past

There have been areas of my life in which I had to make up my mind to walk free from the taskmaster (I am not saying that I am perfect today, because I still deal with things, just as you do). Did you know that you can carry ideas and attitudes over to your Christian walk that you had before you became a Christian? For example, you can carry things into your walk from bad times you have experienced in life long before you were saved. Also, you can have wrong ideas and attitudes based on bad things you have experienced *since* you were saved.

Have you ever experienced bad times since you have been a Christian? No doubt, you have. You still have those memories. A certain fear might exist that those bad things are going to happen again. Right now is the time you must make up your mind, "Bless God, it is *not* going to happen again! God is for me. He's in me, and He is my source. God is going to move in my life. He is going to deliver me and meet my need. I am *loosed* in Jesus' Name!"

You see, it is a decision. The choice is yours.

I can promise that if you hold fast to God and His Word without quitting, God will come through for you, but, as I said, circumstances do not always line up overnight. Sometimes things can appear to get worse before they get better.

I was amazed at the things that occurred in my life when I finally made the decision to quit serving the devil. When Becky and I first started going to church years ago, *immediately,* the devil started stealing from us. We were not even serving God yet; we were just getting into church, but the devil was trying to "nip in the bud" our deliverance and freedom. We had moved to Houston, Texas, and someone stole from the trunk of our car every bit of clothes that Becky owned! Then Becky got sick, and I could not find a job anywhere. Before that, I had a good job making lots of money, but, suddenly, I was living for God, and no one would hire me!

In my entire life, I had never been without a job; I had always been able to find one. But no one wanted to hire me. It was not natural!

What was different in our lives? The only thing we could "put our finger on" was that we had gone to church and decided to turn our lives around! The company I worked for before wanted me to come back, but I did not want to go back. We were obeying God, and we were heading out of Egypt! God was calling us to greater heights, but circumstances in our lives got worse before they got better.

We know that there is a spiritual force arrayed against us. Ephesians 6:12 says, *"For we wrestle not against flesh and blood, but against principalities, against powers, against the rulers of the darkness of this world, against spiritual wickedness in high places."* There are taskmasters — principalities, powers, rulers of the darkness of this world, spiritual wickedness in high places — that want to keep us down and defeated.

Paul had a demon specifically arrayed against him that he called a thorn in the flesh (2 Cor. 12:7). Everywhere Paul went, he had *revival*, but, then, he had *revolt*! One minute he would be preaching to people, and the glory of God would fall. People were saved and healed.

But then the next minute, this or that group would come against him and cast Paul out of the city. Once they stoned him. Just read the Book of Acts. In Athens on Mars Hill, the people one minute thought Paul was a god, and the next minute, they tried to kill him! There were demon spirits trying to push and mold and oppress Paul. They will try to do the same thing to you.

Demon spirits do not care if you live as the world lives and share the world's philosophy. However, the minute you start giving and working for God — the minute you start to walk around free as a bird with no cares — suddenly, you are dangerous to the kingdom of darkness. "Pharaoh," the devil, will tell his taskmasters, "We have to stop them. We have to do something about this bunch!"

So what do you do if "all hell breaks loose"? You just fight the good fight of faith! You stay with it. You do not give up. You expect God to bring deliverance into your life. Deliverance *will* come, and with that deliverance, God will raise you to new levels of faith, glory, and strength. Right now, you may feel as Moses did in Exodus 5:22 and 23. You might be thinking, *Lord, I thought You were going to deliver me. Lord, I thought things were going to get better?* Things *will* get better if you will not quit, because you have a right to be loosed from the taskmaster!

A Taskmaster Mentality Will Hinder
Forward Progress

Many times, our mentality is wrong, and that is what defeats us. Our thinking becomes so clouded by our past experiences and our present circumstances that we do not understand that we are already free!

God sent His Son to destroy the taskmaster. He sent His Spirit to live on the inside of you, to give you anything you need. God is not withholding from you. The taskmaster is just *telling* you that He is. The devil is trying to browbeat you. He knows your weaknesses, but he does not know anything new. He does the same old thing over and over again.

He might put a different dress on it. He might put a different coat of paint or a different design on it, but it is the same thing over and over.

The devil knows what button to push! So turn that sucker off! Then when he pushes your button, nothing will happen! Make up your mind that you are going to be free. Your circumstances may not look a bit different at first, but they will change if you hang in there and will not quit. When you understand and act on the fact that you already have been loosed from the taskmaster, you will be indomitable in your spirit! Your victory cannot be stopped!

Once you make up your mind you are going to be what God says you are and that you are not going to allow the taskmaster to stop or hinder you, there will not be a thing the devil can do about it. When Moses said, "It's time for our people to go," there was not anything Pharaoh could ultimately do but to let them go. Certainly, he put up a good fight. He tried to stop them. He lied. He deceived. He tried everything he could, but in the end, what happened? God's people were free! They should have left that mentality there in Egypt and walked out totally free, but they did not. It hindered their forward progress.

Get Rid of Excess Baggage
That Will Hinder You

I know that when you become saved, you are a new creature in Christ Jesus (2 Cor. 5:17). Old things have passed away. However, in reality, people often bring baggage with them, and they need to deal with it or it will defeat them.

An example of that can be found in the Word of God in a sorcerer named Simon. The Bible says that when Philip preached and started doing all the miracles by the Spirit of God, Simon believed and was baptized (Acts 8:13). In other words, he became *saved* and was baptized. Now Simon the sorcerer had been a "hot-shot." People had lifted him up, treating him as some kind of god — until the real thing came along. (I tell you, New Age and the world do not have anything on us. Some people are so afraid of New Age. They are afraid they will become deceived, but if they attend church every time the doors are open and pray and study their Bible, they will be aware of any deception that tries to come along to ensnare them.)

In Simon the sorcerer's case, when the "true" came on the scene, the "false" looked pitiful! I am not saying that the supernatural things of God cannot be "duplicated" or mimicked. In Exodus, Moses' brother, Aaron, threw down his rod, and it turned into a snake. The magicians for Pharaoh said, "Well, that's no big deal," and they did the same thing. However, something happened after that. *Aaron's snake ate the magicians' snakes! (See* Exodus 7:9-12.) I have always wondered if, after Aaron's snake turned back into a rod, it was bigger than it was before after eating all those other snakes!

Looking at Acts 8:14 and 15, we can see that Peter and John heard about what happened — about Simon and the others receiving Jesus. None of the new converts had received the Holy Ghost yet. So Peter and John went up to pray for them that they had receive the Holy Ghost. (You see, different people have different gifts. No one person can do everything.) They started praying for people, and people started getting baptized in the Holy Ghost.

The Bible does not say specifically what it was that Simon saw, but Simon saw something happening to people when Peter and John laid their hands on them. For one, I know they started speaking in other tongues. And Simon said, in effect, "If I could do what they are doing, I'd be a big-shot again." He offered Peter and John money for the power to do what they were doing.

Simon was not trying to buy the baptism in the Holy Ghost, as some believe. If it were just the baptism in the Holy Ghost that he was after, he could have just waited in line to be prayed for like everyone else! Simon wanted the *power*, and that is where he missed it. The taskmaster that controlled him through pride led him astray. Simon saw the anointing on the lives of Peter and John, and when he saw them laying hands on people, and the people raised their hands and spoke in tongues, he said, "I want that power too. If I had that, everybody would want to come to me." That old taskmaster of the world rose up, and Simon yielded to it. But then Peter "nailed" him, so to speak. Peter said, "You are full of bitterness and iniquity" (vv. 21-23).

Many people wonder what happened to Simon afterward. I believe he repented, because he wanted Peter to pray for him. After Peter rebuked him, Simon said, "Pray for me" (Acts 8:24)

Friend, you can be a Christian and bring baggage with you into your Christian walk that you do not have to have. You can be free of it if you are *willing* to be free.

Old Problems Will Try
To Hold on to a Believer

Here is where the problem comes in, causing Christians to be bound (as a pastor, I have seen this over and over and over again). When you become saved, you do not get a new set of problems. What happens is, what you already have as a problem can become *magnified*.

It's the truth! When you get saved, you do not *want* to do the kind of things you did before. You do not want to act as you did before, but there can be some deep-rooted problems you had before you were saved. If you do not deal with those things, they will bind you up more when you get saved then they ever did before you got saved. You can hide those problems in the lust of the flesh. You can hide them in irresponsibility. You can hide them in other ways — in actions that are not wrong in and of themselves, such as eating, but your appetite could be out of control.

Maybe there are some things that have not changed since you became saved. You are dealing with the same burdens you had before you were saved. You are bound with the same problem, only now it seems as if it is magnified. You are not alone. Just realize that Satan, not God, is the binder and that God wants you to be free. He has made a way for you to be free through His Son Jesus.

I see examples of people's failure to deal with past burdens in many areas, including the area of divorce and remarriage. I see people who have been married two or three times in the world, and when they become saved, they do the same thing!

I also see people who lied and were very dishonest before they became saved. And when they became saved, they just kept on lying. They did not deal with it. They did not understand that there was a taskmaster who was going to try to burden them and hold them down. They were not willing to deal with their problem and break its power over their lives.

It is so important that you realize these facts and that you apply yourself to do something about them. The taskmaster is real, and he will see to it that you are bound for the rest of your life if you let him. So learn to stand against him and believe God and His Word.

We know that we can not only be loosed from the taskmaster, but we can also get rid of a wrong mentality — wrong thinking — from the past that will hinder us and keep us from rising to great heights in our walk with God!

Chapter 4
Eleven Freedom Principles
Part 1

In Chapter 1, we looked at three taskmasters from Exodus 1: the chief of tribute, the chief of burdens, and the chief of works. I said that the devil appoints taskmasters over God's people, Christians, today, but we have a covenant right to be free — *loosed* from the taskmaster! In this chapter, we will look at principles you need to know to be delivered from these taskmasters.

As a believer, a child of God, you can be loosed from whatever binds you. However, just because you go to church does not mean that you are going to be loosed. Going to church is good and right, but going to church in itself does not set you at liberty.

It is a good start, but attending church is not what looses you from the taskmaster. Yet you can know that Jesus wants you to be free. God wants you to be loosed! You have a right to it, because you have a covenant with Him.

I shared with you from Exodus 1 about the taskmasters of Egypt that were appointed over the children of Israel, because I believe it is a pattern of bondage that the enemy uses today. The Bible says that we are to look at the children of Israel as examples (1 Cor. 10:11) — not as examples of being bound but of how to be free!

The devil and the world do not want you to be free, because the minute you become free, you are going to have authority over the world. You are not going to have authority *in* the world, but you are going to have authority *over* the world and its ways. It will not be able to control or dominate you and dictate how you should live — what you do, how you do it, what you eat, where you sleep, and so forth.

I believe there is a financial boom, a financial blessing, coming to the Church, because we are breaking the yoke of the taskmaster concerning finances. I believe finances are going to flow into the Body of Christ so they can flow out to the world in the spreading of the Good News, the Gospel. I do not believe it is going to come by the wisdom of man or because someone in the church becomes a whiz in the stock market and makes millions of dollars. No, it is going to be supernatural. And when the world hands it over, they will not even know why they are doing it!

The reason why most Christians do not have money is because the chief of *tribute* is binding them. So you have to break that yoke off your life.

Too many people, especially in this country, are bound by the chief of *works*. They are so busy, they do not have time for church. What are they busy with? *Stuff!*

For example, perhaps you used to be able to get up and relax a little bit on Saturday morning and maybe read the newspaper. However, for many, Saturday today is a day to do *stuff*. They're busy doing this, that, and the other thing, and the next thing they know, it is dark!

Have you ever been there? If you are not careful, the taskmaster will keep you so busy working that you will not have time for God. You will not have time for contact with what you really need in life — your source of grace and power — the Presence of God.

At some point, you need to draw the line. Some people will say, "Yes, but I have to provide for my family." Certainly, you need to provide for your family.

Some people at the other extreme will say, "Oh, good, I can quit my job, and God is just going to take care of my family." I am not telling you to quit your job. I am just saying that your job does not need to consume you.

As I already mentioned, a third taskmaster that wants to control us in the chief of *burdens*. You remember the taskmasters kept the Israelites so oppressed, beaten down, and downtrodden that they did not have a good image of themselves anymore. The taskmasters killed their babies and oppressed them with difficulties and just made their lives miserable to the point the Israelites did not see themselves as worthy of living life, especially a *good* life.

You know, in America, we have the highest suicide rate in the world. We are the most prosperous nation in the world, but the ones who are committing suicide are not predominantly from ghettos and economically depressed communities. No, it is predominantly the ones with money in their pockets who are doing it. The taskmaster is oppressing them. They have things, but life is not enjoyable. They do not enjoy life.

Someone might say, "Well, *I'm* not bound, because I don't have any money!" However, people in that category can be the world's worst at being bound, because they are trying anything and everything to get money, or they are busy being jealous over what someone else has.

You have to make up your mind to resist the devil, and he will flee (James 4:7). You must make up your mind, "Bless God, I am not going to live average. I am not going to live the way everyone else does — the way the world tells me to live. I am going to live for God, and I am going to rise up high in Him and get into the flow of what He wants for my life."

When you do that, things will start changing! The things of the world and the circumstances of life will grow dim to you, and the glory of God will grow brighter and brighter and brighter!

In this chapter, I want to share with you some things you need to know to be delivered from the taskmaster. I call them freedom principles, because they are things that God did for Israel and dealt with them about when He delivered them from Egypt. I believe that if *you* will begin to put these principles into practice in your life, you will be delivered from the taskmaster and rise to a new level of living in the blessings of God.

Freedom Principle Number One: Receive a Revelation of Your New Beginning

The first thing you need in order to be loosed from the taskmaster is a new beginning. There has to be a point where you say, "This is the beginning. I'm going to do it today. I am going to begin today to be free of debt, cares, and worries. I'm going to be loosed so I can do something for God. My deliverance starts *now!*"

A new beginning is not mentally setting a date on which you will be free. No, it is acting on the revelation that God wants you to be free and has made a way for you to be free from *anything* that binds you.

Again, I am using the children of Israel as an example. This time, we need to look at their deliverance from Egypt as a reference.

EXODUS 12:1,2
1 And the Lord spake unto Moses and Aaron in the land of Egypt; saying,
2 This month shall be unto you the BEGINNING of months: it shall be the first month of the year to you.

Deliverance starts in the realm of the Spirit when you make the decision to be free. You may not see anything at first.

Even with the children of Israel, deliverance started first in the Spirit. Before you ever see your deliverance on the outside, you have to first receive the *revelation* of your deliverance and let it explode in your spirit. You have to have it on the *inside*!

You need to know on the inside that God has given you a word and that He has spoken to you. It could be when hands are laid on you, when you are reading the Word, or maybe when you receive a prophecy or a word of knowledge. When that happens, something on the inside of you says, "Bless God, this is it. I'm going to be free. I'm going to be delivered. I am going to be *loosed* from this taskmaster." It starts on the inside, and it is a new beginning.

Let us look at another one of my favorite verses.

ISAIAH 43:19,20
19 Behold, I will do a NEW THING; now it shall spring forth; shall ye not know it? I will even make a way in the wilderness, and rivers in the desert.
20 The beast of the field shall honour me, the dragons and the owls: because I give waters in the wilderness, and rivers in the desert, to give drink to my people, my chosen.

God said, "I will do a new thing; it shall spring forth." Listen, friend, you do not want "stale manna." You do not want yesterday's revelation. Now I am not saying that yesterday's revelation is of no use today, but you want God speaking to you *now* — right where you are today — in your present situation and circumstance. You need to say, "Lord, right now, where are we going? This is a new day." And as you seek Him, you will get a new beginning.

Mark Off the Old and Start the New

You could just make a dividing line, so speak, and say, "That is old; this is new." That is what happens when you became saved: *"Therefore if any man be in Christ, he is a new creature: old things are passed away; behold, all things are become new"* (2 Cor. 5:17). You need to carry this truth over into your spiritual life and make new beginnings. Mark off the old and start the new in areas of your life where you have been bound.

The first thing God told the children of Israel to do in preparation for their deliverance was: "I want you to mark it down on your calendar: 'This is a new beginning.' You have been in bondage. You have been held down. You have been bound up, but this is a new beginning."

In your own life, when you get that on the inside of you, it does not matter what the world says. It does not matter what the circumstances say, because a new beginning is coming!

I want to share a "new beginning" story involving a friend of mine who, years ago, was a farmer. My friend went to college, and he got married while he was in college. He and his wife had a baby. After he graduated, his heart's desire was to go to law school. In his heart, he really wanted to be a lawyer, so he enrolled.

He related: "The first day of my first semester of law school, I walked into the classroom, and fear just enveloped me. I thought, *What am I going to do? I've got a wife and baby at home, and I can't take care of them. I'm going to be in law school for the next few years. What am I going to do to take care of my family? I'm going to lose them.'"

So my friend quit law school. He went back and worked on the family farm and did well taking care of the farm. He got saved and filled with the Holy Ghost (my wife and I had the privilege of praying with him). He and his wife had another child, and they bought a home. They were prospering.

One night in a church service, the Lord spoke to my friend about returning to law school. Now my friend had already started a family, but when God spoke to him, it went off inside him like a light. It was a revelation from God of what he was supposed to do. The man was nearly thirty years old and had been out of school for more than six years, but God was giving him a new beginning.

Do you know what my friend did? He packed up his family and went back to college! He didn't know how God was going to provide for them, but he knew what he had heard God say. My friend just said, "This is a new beginning. This is what I should have done, and this is what I'm going to do." So his wife, who had always been interested in real estate, took some real estate courses and started selling real estate, and she began doing well. The family was taken care of while he went to law school. In fact, they flourished! All of their needs were met, and he did not even have to work while he was in school.

Later, he told me that the first day of law school the second time around, he walked into that same classroom, and the same fear came on him! Why? Because those taskmasters do not like to let go! However, now he had something to fight with. So he said, "Devil, this is a new beginning. I am doing what I ought to do and what you stole from me. I am going to stay here, and I am going to finish law school. I'm *going* to do what I know God told me to do!"

My friend went through law school and made straight A's. When he graduated, he returned to his hometown, which was just a little country town. They only had three lawyers in the whole town, and one of the lawyers there asked him to go into business with him as a junior partner. Now my friend had just graduated from law school, and he was about thirty-two years old. He said, "Well, I want to live here, and this is the only opportunity I have right now. I don't know enough to get out on my own." So he went to work for this other lawyer.

The man he went into partnership with turned out to have some moral problems. And after a while, my friend did not want to be involved with this man anymore, particularly because of the way the man had dealt with some things he had done wrong that had been exposed. My friend was also concerned about losing all of their clients. So he said, "Well, I'm going to go out and just try it on my own." He opened his own practice — a one-room office — and every one of their clients came over to him! Within a year's time he had to hire someone to help him. God had put him in the same position he would have been in if he had not allowed the devil to rob him of his opportunity to attend law school years before. God restored *everything* to him because he was willing to have a new beginning.

That taskmaster, the devil, was trying to hold my friend back to keep him from being what God wanted him to be — and the devil got away with it for five or six years! However, one day, the revelation went off in his heart, "This is a new day. God is going to do a new thing. It's a new beginning." When it did, he just stepped out by faith, and God began to work amazing things in his life.

Think about what would have happened if my friend had not gone back to law school. He would have been fifty years old and still farming. (There's nothing wrong with farming. However, if it is not what God wants you to do, it is wrong.) Today he is a successful lawyer and well respected in the community, because he made up his mind, "I'm not going to let the devil control me. I'm going to be loosed from this burden, and I'm going to do what God called me to do." God loosed him from that taskmaster and gave him a new beginning!

Anyone living in this world can have a new beginning. That means *you* can have a new beginning. It does not matter what you have done or have not done. It does not matter how bad off you are or what mess you think your life has become. God will give you a new beginning. You can be loosed from the taskmaster!

Freedom Principle Number Two:
Be Obedient to the Terms of the Sacrifice

God gave the children of Israel specific instructions about the Passover sacrifice when they were preparing to be delivered from Egypt. The second thing *you* must do to free yourself from the taskmaster is to be willing and obedient to what God tells *you* to do.

EXODUS 12:3-10
3 Speak ye unto all the congregation of Israel, saying, In the tenth day of this month they shall take to them every man a lamb, according to the house of their fathers, a lamb for an house:
4 And if the household be too little for the lamb, let him and his neighbour next unto his house take it according to the number of the souls; every man according to his eating shall make your count for the lamb.
5 Your lamb shall be without blemish, a male of the first year: ye shall take it out from the sheep, or from the goats:
6 And ye shall keep it until the fourteenth day of the same month: and the whole assembly of the congregation of Israel shall kill it in the evening.
7 And they shall take of the blood, and strike it on the two side posts and on the upper doorpost of the houses, wherein they shall eat it.
8 And they shall eat the flesh in that night, roast with fire, and unleavened bread; and with bitter herbs they shall eat it.
9 Eat not of it raw, nor sodden at all with water, but roast with fire; his head with his legs, and with the purtenance thereof.
10 And ye shall let nothing of it remain until the morning; and that which remaineth of it until the morning ye shall burn with fire.

To obtain their deliverance, Israel had to be obedient to the instructions in these verses regarding the sacrifice. In much the same way, *you* have to be obedient to the sacrifice to obtain the deliverance that *you* desire. You have to be obedient to what God tells you to do.

Now in the case of my lawyer friend, he could have said, "Well, you know, I'm just going to *dream* about going to law school. I'm going to *think* about it. Maybe God will do something." But my friend had to do more than that. God had already spoken. My friend had to be obedient. *He* had to move and act on what God told him to do.

The same is true in your life if you want everything that God has for you. You can't just say, "God, why don't You *do* something!" God might want *you* to do something! When God tells you something, and it seems a little different or even difficult, you can not just sit down and say, "I'm not going to do it." If you are not obedient to the sacrifices, you will never be free from the taskmaster.

There have been several times in the area of finances when my wife and I have struggled — when we did not know how we were going to make it. There have been times when the church we pastor struggled financially. I would pray and seek God, and He would say, "Give."

I would say, "No, Lord, You don't understand. I need to *get*."

But the Lord would say, "Give," and back and forth we would go! I would say, "Lord, I don't need to *give*; I need to *get*."

"No, I want you to give."

"Get," I would respond.

"Give."

"Get."

"Give!"

You know, the Lord will not relent concerning His will for you. So, after a while, I would say, "Okay," and Becky and I would give. We would sow seed. We would take something that was very valuable to us, and we would sell it for money to give, or we would just give away the valuable item. We have done that many times. I am not lifting us up. I am just telling you something that works. (You have to do it in obedience to God, not just to be doing it.)

Our church has done the same thing. We have sown into other ministries when we did not really have the money to give, so we had to sacrifice in other areas. Yet, gradually, as we obeyed God in the area of finances, it broke the yoke of the taskmaster over us, because we were acting in obedience. When you are obedient spiritually, God will begin to move. God will begin to do supernatural things because you are obedient to the sacrifice.

Faith Actions Change the Spirit World

The devil does not want you to give, because he is the chief of tribute, and he wants to keep you bound financially. However, one way he *cannot* control you is in the area of your giving. I have given in good times; I have given when I have had more than enough, but I have also given in bad times, when I did not have enough. Why? Because I wanted to be obedient to the sacrifice and break the yoke of the taskmaster in my life. You see, *faith actions change the spirit world.* Faith actions set the will of God in motion in your life!

You have to be obedient to the sacrifice. The children of Israel put that blood on the door posts in obedience to the Lord. When they did, it separated them in the spiritual realm from the Egyptians. Certainly, anyone can be religious and talk a good game, but it is only the obedient children of God who are going to actually "put the blood on the door posts." In other words, they are going to *act*. They are going to obey.

When you act in obedience to God, you separate yourself from the rest of the world. Rhetorical talk and religious gibberish do not separate you. *Acting* separates you. In other words, you can *talk* about missions all you want. You can even *cry* over the world all you want, but until you obey God and *act* on missions in the way that God wants you to, you are no different than the world.

If you are going to be loosed, you have to be obedient to the sacrifice. You cannot act like the world and receive from God. Notice God told the children of Israel in Exodus 12:8 and 9, "I want you to *roast* the meat." Do you know why God said that? Because the Egyptians ate theirs raw to worship their gods. That is why God said, "Do it exactly the way I tell you to." He told them to do it in just the opposite way as the Egyptians did it. Similarly, God is going to tell you to do things in just the opposite way as the world does them.

If we are not careful, we might listen to some well-meaning Christians who say, "Now be reasonable. Be sensible about this." In other words, what they are saying is, "Be *worldly* about this"! Many times God will tell you to do something that is contrary to the world's way of thinking, and you are going to have to obey Him if you want the blessing.

Becky and I have another friend who is president of another well-known ministry. It is amazing to me how many well-meaning people, including bankers and business professionals, have tried to tell her how to run her ministry. They cannot believe that she does it just through contributions. They ask her, "Don't you have a benefactor? Don't you have some endowment to help you?"

She says, "No, we just believe God to pay the bills."

The World Is Clueless!

The world does not understand that. They do not have a clue how that can be possible! God wants us to do things His way, not the world's way. It seems the minute you start getting in line with the way the world does things, God says, "Roast that sucker! Do it differently."

For example, someone might come to you and say, "Could you loan me ten dollars?" You might say, "Well, that sounds reasonable. Sure, I'll loan you ten dollars."

However, did you know that is not what the Bible says you ought to do? The Bible says you ought to *give* it to him (Matt. 5:42).

Now I am not telling you to always be giving people money when they ask for it. My point is, we do not do things the way the world does; we *give*.

"What if they don't pay it back?" someone asked. Well, they just don't pay it back. Trust me, God will repay you when you are obedient to the sacrifice, even though it is different.

God is going to do things differently than the world does them. Often, God will not do things *through* the world either. I have actually heard people say, "I just wish Elvis would have gotten saved before he died. Just think how many people he could have reached for Jesus!" If Elvis had begun proclaiming Jesus, he would have become a fool in the world's eyes, just as we are! God does not do things the world's way.

The world has some funny ideas. They do not understand spiritual things. For example, news reporters have wanted to interview me. They wanted me to explain our success. I do not try to explain that, because they are not going to understand it. I just let them figure it out for themselves. Also, they will want me to explain the "social ramifications of our church philosophy whereby we are able to have a racially integrated congregation."

They are looking for something complicated, but I tell them, "We are all one in Jesus. There is no color; there is no race. We are all one people, and when we come together to worship Jesus, that is all we're looking at — Jesus the Savior of *all* the world!"

Freedom Principle Number Three: Be Prepared for Change

The third freedom principle you will need to put into practice to be loosed from the taskmaster is, you are going to have to be prepared for change.

EXODUS 12:11
11 And thus shall ye eat it [the Passover lamb]; with your loins girded, your shoes on your feet, and your staff in your hand; and ye shall eat it in haste: it is the Lord's passover.

God told the children of Israel to get ready to move. Things were going to change in their lives, and God was getting them ready for it.

You know, some people are always expecting God to do something for them, but then when He does it, it just blows their mind. For example, I know ladies who prayed for years for their husbands to be saved. Then when the man goes to the altar to be saved and filled with the Holy Ghost, instead of getting glad, the wife gets mad! Why? Because, all of a sudden, he knows a little something spiritually. He is the spiritual head of the house. And she is not quite ready for it.

I see this happen all the time. So when you are expecting God to do something — when you are expecting a deliverance from the taskmaster — you had better do it with your "loins girded, your shoes on your feet, and your staff in your hand"! You had better be ready to go, so to speak, because God is going to bring a deliverance! When He does, you need to be able to run with it. You need to be prepared for change.

I knew a man years ago whose wife used to turn in prayer requests for his salvation, and we as a church would pray for him. Then one day, he got saved. I remember him coming into my office, just weeping. "Oh, Brother Sam, it's real. It's so real." This man was excited, but he would not let go of his old unsaved friends.

You see, he was not ready to change. Do you know what? He is not in church anymore. His old friends have him doing things with them. He is still doing the things he used to do.

When you are loosed, you had better do things differently if you do not want to go back to being bound!

I know people who have seen financial miracles in their lives. They were in debt up to their eyeballs! They owed every credit card company you could think of. God supernaturally delivered them, but, six months later, they owed money again to the same credit card companies — because they did not change. As I said, when you are loosed, you had better be prepared to change! God wants us to change!

The Bible says we are being changed from "glory to glory" (2 Cor. 3:18). We are moving forward — we are changing! Once you make up your mind to change, God will bring deliverance in your life. He will loose you from the taskmaster.

Freedom Principle Number Four:
Expect a Supernatural Sign

Freedom principle number four also can be found in Exodus chapter 12: *Expect a supernatural sign.*

EXODUS 12:13
13 And the blood shall be to you for a TOKEN [or sign] upon the houses where ye are: and when I see the blood, I will pass over you, and the plague shall not be upon you to destroy you, when I smite the land of Egypt.

Many times, Christians, especially we faith people, like to say, "We aren't moved by what we see. We don't need anything; we walk by faith." However, I personally like it when God shows me something and speaks to me. I found out that God will do that! I am not talking about putting "a fleece" out before God, such as when Gideon sought the Lord to make the fleece wet for a "yes" answer and dry for a "no" answer (Judges 6:37). Some people put out fleeces today, saying, "Lord, if You want me to have this job, when I go in, they'll hire me. If they don't, I'll know You don't want me to work there."

That is not how God wants us to be led. He wants us to be led by His Spirit.

So when I refer to a supernatural sign, that is not what I am talking about, but I do want to tell you that when God begins to direct you out of bondage, He will give you a sign. He will reveal things to you. He will show you things, as the Bible says He did for the children of Israel: *"And the blood shall be to you for a token upon the houses where ye are: and when I see the blood, I will pass over you, and the plague shall not be upon you to destroy you, when I smite the land of Egypt"* (Exod. 12:13).

God certainly showed them a sign. The death angel that killed all of the Egyptians' firstborn was a sign to them because it did not touch their houses which were covered with the lamb's blood. God will always perform what He speaks!

Let me give you a specific example. Someone will say to me, "God spoke to me to go on a missions trip." I will say, "That's wonderful. How much is it going to cost?"

The person tells me, "Such-and-such amount," and I will ask him, "Well, do you have the money?"

"No, I'm believing God for the money."

I will ask, "That is great. Has anyone felt a witness in his spirit to help you with this?"

"Well, no. Everyone I talk to tells me I shouldn't go, but I'm going anyway."

Well, the time comes for the trip, and the person does not have the money to go. He makes some kind of excuse about why he is not going, but if he would just be honest about it, if God were in it, there would have been some signs along the way. Someone would have blessed him financially. Someone would have helped and encouraged him. There would have been a sign along the way — a supernatural sign. I mean, God would have done something!

Years ago God spoke to me to go on a missions trip. I had not been saved very long, and I was believing God for the money. We were going to leave on a Thursday, and that Wednesday night at church, I just knew my pastor, Brother John Osteen, was going to get up and take up an offering for me to go on that missions trip! I did not have the money, but, you know, the strangest thing happened. Pastor Osteen did not take up an offering, but that night before I was going to leave, there was a knock on my front door. It was a certain preacher who said, "God spoke to me to bring you this money for your missions trip." It was exactly how much I needed! Then he added, "The Lord just wanted you to know that you're supposed to go on this trip."

That was a sign!

Signs Along the Way

When God is ministering to you, He will reveal a sign to you along the way. It may be through the Word. I have had people in my services come up to me many, many times and say, "Brother Sam, I've been believing God in a certain area, and that message you preached today was exactly what I needed to hear!"

That was a sign, because God will always confirm what He is saying and what He is doing. He will bring a confirmation to you.

Jesus said something about signs in Mark 16.

MARK 16:17-20
17 And these signs shall follow them that believe; In my name shall they cast out devils; they shall speak with new tongues;
18 They shall take up serpents; and if they drink any deadly thing, it shall not hurt them; they shall lay hands on the

sick, and they shall recover.
19 So then after the Lord had spoken unto them, he was received up into heaven, and sat on the right hand of God.
20 And they went forth, and preached every where, the Lord working with them, and confirming the word WITH SIGNS FOLLOWING. Amen.

Someone might say, "I have a healing ministry."

Are people getting healed?

"Well, not yet."

Maybe that person does not have a healing ministry, because, if he did, it would be confirmed with signs following.

Someone else might say, "I'm called to pastor."

Where are your sheep?

"Well, I don't have any."

Do you understand what I'm saying? There will be signs following a person's ministry. God will confirm it when He is bringing someone a deliverance. Anytime you are believing God and you release your faith, expecting to be delivered, God will confirm it! He will bring a word, and there will be signs following. There will be a supernatural work and a supernatural deliverance. He will always confirm what He is doing. He told the Israelites, "You put that blood on the door posts. I will show you your deliverance."

Then that death angel swept through those cities, and the firstborn children of Egypt were stricken dead. I am sure the Israelites heard all the wailing and crying. When they did, they knew something was about to happen. They knew God was doing something. They had a sign.

Many times people will come up to the front of the church

who need deliverance or healing, so I will lay hands on them. Often when I do, the power of God will go into them and knock them down! I've seen people shake and laugh and do all sorts of things by the Spirit of God. Those are signs. God is working. God is doing something in those people's lives. He will confirm what He does through supernatural signs. You ought to expect it. You should expect God to do something supernatural.

Freedom Principle Number Five: **Put Spiritual Things First**

The fifth freedom principle you are going to have to act on to be loosed from the taskmaster is the principle of putting spiritual things first.

> **EXODUS 12:16,17**
> **16 And in the first day there shall be an holy convocation, and in the seventh day there shall be an holy convocation to you; no manner of work shall be done in them, save that which every man must eat, that only may be done of you.**
> **17 And ye shall observe the feat of unleavened bread; for in this selfsame day have I brought your armies out of the land of Egypt: therefore shall ye observe this day in your generations by an ordinance for ever.**

In verse 16, the Lord commanded Israel, saying, *"...in the first day there shall be an holy convocation...."* In this verse, God was telling the children of Israel, as He is telling His Church today, "If you want to be delivered, put spiritual things first."

So God told the children of Israel to have a holy convocation. He was saying, "Come on. Let's have *church*"! That word "convocation" in this verse means *a called-out time with God* or *a separated time with God.* So if God is going to bring deliverance in your life, you are going to need those called-out times with God.

Now that word "convocation" also means *public meeting.* And that means *church!* Church is certainly a holy convocation. It is a called-out time. When you go to church, you separate yourself from the operation of the world. You are saying, "I am going to separate myself from the world, and I'm going to come before God with fellow believers to worship Him and hear His Word."

First Things First

You have to put spiritual things first if you want to receive deliverance in your life. If God is going to do something in your life, you have to put Him first. I am amazed at the number of people I have heard say, "I'd go to church tonight, but I'd really rather go do something else." You can do that, because that is your business, but if you do, do not wonder why you are not getting deliverance — why God is not moving in your life. You are not willing to have called-out times with Him.

I am not trying to make you feel condemned. I am simply saying that there has to be those called-out times with God. You need to put first things first and be involved with spiritual things, such as praying, reading your Bible, fellowshipping with God, and going to church!

The first thing God said when He brought the children out of Egypt was, "Get ready, because from now on, we are going to have some time together. We are going to have some called-out times, some public meetings." We need to learn from that to put spiritual things first.

I believe the closer we get to the end of time and the time of Jesus' return, the more valuable it is going to be for us to come together. We need to shake off the filth of the world and worship and glorify God together as local church families.

I remember years ago when I had been saved less than two years, Becky's sister and brother-in-law came to visit us. We had been praying and really believing God for their salvation. When they arrived, my brother-in-law and I began talking about playing golf. So we decided that instead of going to church, we were going to play golf.

(For months afterward, my wife didn't say anything, but I knew she was not happy about it. I rationalized that I did not get to see my brother-in-law that often, so when I did get to see him, I wanted to play a little golf.)

So Becky and her sister went to church that day, and my brother-in-law and I went to play golf, but I was miserable the entire time. I did not enjoy it! Becky and I usually did not miss church. We *still* do not miss church. We go to church, even when we are not preaching! Why? Because you need those called-out times with God. (I realize now how valuable that called-out time could have been that day as I was out there on the course chasing that little white ball!)

Today my brother-in-law is serving God. He loves God. However, to this day, I cannot help thinking about what kind of impression I must have made on him! I was the saved one, yet I would rather play golf than go to church! That bothered me for the longest time.

Attending church is not a religious ritual. It is an important time of separation, a time of being called out. It speaks to others of who you really are. Certainly, others may laugh at you and mock you and call you a "religious nut," but I believe that when they do, deep down on the inside, they are really wishing they had what you have.

Putting spiritual things first will have to happen in your life if you want to be free from the taskmaster. If you are ever going to rise up higher and break free of the chains of bondage, you are going to have to put the things of God above all else.

Freedom principle number six goes right along with principle number five concerning the holy convocation or called-out time that God commanded the children of Israel to have. It has to do with putting spiritual things first.

Freedom Principle Number Six: Worship God for Your Deliverance

Worship is a powerful tool of deliverance that God uses to set His people free from the enemy, the taskmaster, who tries to bind them. God used this tool in the case of the children of Israel, and He uses that same principle today.

> **EXODUS 12:26,27**
> **26 And it shall come to pass, when your children shall say unto you, What mean ye by this service?**
> **27 ...It is the sacrifice of the Lord's passover, who passed over the houses of the children of Israel in Egypt, when he smote the Egyptians, and delivered our houses. And the people bowed the head and WORSHIPPED.**

One of the easiest ways to be set free from any problem in your life is to worship God. I do not mean to just sing hymns *about* God or songs *about* His deliverance. I am talking about the true worship of God, from the heart. I do not mean just in church. You need to worship God in your private time, lifting up your hands before Him. You can even worship the Lord in your automobile. You can have quiet time, just you and the Lord, and you can worship Him, magnifying and glorifying His Name. You can begin to lift up your voice, and worship will rise up out of your spirit.

Worship in church ought to be something that is just an extension of our daily worship of God. So just lift up your voice before the Lord and begin to worship, magnify, and glorify Him!

Someone said, "But, Pastor Carr, I can't sing!"

So what if you can't sing! Worship does not have to do with singing. It has to do with *worship*.

There was a time when I personally never thought I could worship God because I could not sing. That was my equation! I believed, "If you can't sing, you can't worship."

However, I discovered that when I was alone with God, I could not really hear myself anyway, so it did not matter to me, and it certainly didn't matter to God.

Worship Will Lift the Burdens of Your Life

The Lord told me something significant about this principle once. He said, "Worship will lift the burdens of your life." That is powerful! If you will get in the Presence of God and worship Him, those burdens that are wearing you down and holding you down will begin to be lifted from you. They will begin to just float away as you worship God and magnify God.

You can worship God for your deliverance. You can worship God and say, "Oh, thank You, Lord, for I am delivered. I just worship You. You are my God. Thank You, Lord, that I'm delivered. I just want to praise You. I just want to worship You. I want to glorify You because I know You are my God and my deliverer."

Your worship of God doesn't have to be some well-oiled, fine-tuned symphony, because that is not what God hears anyway. God hears the heart. And when you begin to worship God from you heart, it brings deliverance in your life.

I will tell you, there have been several times since I have been saved when I underwent tremendous difficulty and adversity. Many times, I would get before God in my church sanctuary alone in the middle of the night. I would walk around the sanctuary with my hands lifted, just worshipping God and thanking Him for deliverance. And I never walked out of that place without having my burden lifted and without seeing God's deliverance.

God will do the same for you, but if you are going to experience deliverance from the taskmaster, it is important that you learn to worship God and put spiritual things first.

Chapter 5
Eleven Freedom Principles
Part 2

You know, some people need to be delivered from the taskmaster, but they are not really ready to receive. They think they are, but they are not. You have to be *prepared* to receive whatever it is you need from God.

Freedom Principle Number Seven:
Be Ready To Receive

The seventh thing you are going to have to do to be loosed from your bondage is, you are going to have to be ready to receive!

One of the reasons people are not ready to receive is, they have to receive the way God tells them to receive, and they cannot handle that. They do not want to do that. For example, I know people who believed God for money, but when someone came up to them and tried to give them some money, they said, "Oh, no. I can't accept that."

They were thinking the money was going to come through a different channel than the one God prepared for them. So they were not ready to receive.

EXODUS 12:35,36
35 And the children of Israel did according to the word of Moses; and they borrowed of the Egyptians jewels of silver, and jewels of gold, and raiment:
36 And the Lord gave the people favour in the sight of the

**Egyptians, so that they lent unto them such things as they
required. And they spoiled the Egyptians.**

Now if you do not read this passage correctly, you will think,
*Well, God just stole from the Egyptians. They borrowed it and
never paid it back.* But the word "borrowed" in this passage does
not mean they borrowed as you would borrow money at a bank
for which you would sign a promissory or demand note. No, the
word "borrowed" here means *asked.*

Now look at what it says in Exodus chapter 3, because God
spoke to Moses specifically about this.

EXODUS 3:21,22
**21 And I will give this people favour in the sight of the Egyp-
tians: and it shall come to pass, that, when ye go, ye shall not go
empty:
22 But every woman shall borrow of her neighbour, and of her
that sojourneth in her house, jewels of silver, and jewels of gold,
and raiment: and ye shall put them upon your sons, and upon
your daughters; and ye shall spoil the Egyptians.**

I like to read verse 21 this way: "I will give this people favor
in the sight of the world, and it shall come to pass that when you
go, you shall not go empty"! That word "empty" in the Hebrew
implies, "You will not go undeserved." The root word is *worthless.*

Some people do not think they are *worthy* to receive. They say,
"That is fine for some people, but God would not do something
like that for me, Pastor Carr." Oh, yes, He would! He would bring
deliverance to you.

"But don't you think I'm asking too much? Don't you think I'm
expecting too much?"

No, and when you walk out delivered, you will not feel
worthless; you won't feel "undeserved."

The Israelites had been in bondage when God gave them these freedom principles. We do not know exactly how long they had been in bondage, but it was for at least eighty to a hundred years. Of course, they had been in Egypt for more than four hundred years, but they had not been in bondage that entire time.

So when the children of Israel "spoiled" the Egyptians by asking for silver and gold, all God was doing was giving them back pay! They had worked all those years for free! So God was not being unjust. He was giving them what they deserved.

You Are Worthy!

Sometimes I look at myself and my life, and I say, "I do not deserve what God has done in my life." Well, the truth is, I *don't*! None of us "deserve" God's goodness and what He has done for us. That is what the grace of God is all about. So where do you draw the line between what you do and do not deserve? I have a "reminder" scripture when I question whether I deserve some blessing from God.

ROMANS 8:32
32 He that spared not his own Son, but delivered him up for us all, how shall he not with him also freely give us all things?

You see, I did not deserve God's Son, and I do not deserve anything else, either. However, since God gave His Son for me, He will give me anything else I want or need — because He already gave His best in giving His Son!

So when God begins to minister to you, deliver you, and bring liberty in an area of your life, don't start wondering whether you really deserve it or not, or you will lose it. The Lord has had to deal with me about that in some areas. I am not worthless and undeserving, and neither are you.

God will work a tremendous deliverance in your life if you just know how to receive. You see, the children of Israel simply *asked* the Egyptians for their silver and gold! They did not feel worthless or undeserving. The Lord said, "You are not going to go empty. You are not going to go undeserved or worthless."

They just walked right in there and said, "I'd like to have these jewels"!

So the Egyptians said, "Sure. Sure. Okay."

Then the Egyptian people probably said, "Why am I giving them these things?"

I believe that in the coming days, God is going to promote many Christians on their jobs, and their boss is going to say, "Why did I give him that?" And Christians are going to say, "Why *did* he give me that?"

When it happens to you — you had better receive it! You deserve it, not because of you, but because of the Deliverer!

Friend, we had better learn how to receive, because I believe God is going to give us opportunities to spoil the "Egyptians" — the world! I don't know how. I don't know when, but I believe there are going to be times when the world is going to do things for us, and, just like the Egyptians, they are going to say, "Why did we do that? We do not understand that. We shouldn't have done that!"

We are not going to walk out empty!

Some people have lost their blessings, because God started blessing them ,and they said, "Oh, I don't deserve that. I'd better be cautious about this blessing. After all, maybe I shouldn't be so blessed."

God said, "Okay, I will find someone who will receive it."

You are not worthless or undeserving. Get hold of that fact in your spirit and be prepared to receive from the Lord. Say out loud: "I'm not going out empty! I'm not going to do it in my own ability, but God has chosen me in Christ! I'm worthy and deserving, and I'm ready to receive what God wants for my life!"

Freedom Principle Number Eight:
Know That the Lord Will Go
Before You and Make a Way!

God wants you to know that He will go before you and make a way. Actually, a way has already been made for your deliverance. You might ask, "Well, where is it? Where is my deliverance?" I don't know, but it is there! God said it was.

Let's look again at Exodus 13.

EXODUS 13:21,22
21 And the Lord went before them by day in a pillar of a cloud, to lead them the way; and by night in a pillar of fire, to give them light; to go by day and night:
22 He took not away the pillar of the cloud by day, nor the pillar of fire by night, from before the people.

The Lord always went before the children of Israel; He was out there before them. That is where your deliverance is — out there before you. God has already prepared it. You just need to follow Him. All you have to do is let the Lord go before you. Then receive your deliverance!

Years ago, I had a pastor friend who got into sin. Now I love this man, and I did everything I could to try to help him get his life right, but I just couldn't because He wasn't willing. He left his wife and his family for another woman. His church "split" into a dozen pieces! So he tried to start another church with this other woman, and it did not work. He finally got into more illicit sin and gross immorality. He ended up in homosexuality. It was sickening all the things he got into. He walked off into total darkness.

One day I received a newsletter in the mail from a certain church, and, as I was looking through it, I saw this man's name in the newsletter. He was working in a local church. I got so excited, I picked up the phone and called the church to ask about him. Sure enough, it was my friend. He was working at this church, and I learned that he was planning to move back down into my part of the country. I did not know it at the time, but he had cancer, so he was moving back home.

He didn't live in my state, but he called me one day and asked if we could have lunch. So he came to see me, and I could tell things had changed in his life and that his heart was right with God.

As we were sitting there at lunch, I asked him, "Tell me your story. Tell me what happened."

So he told me about all the sinful things he had gotten into. He had gone to the depths of sexual perversion; he had been all bound up. He said he came home one day, and the girl he had left his wife for had gone. She took everything and left. My friend said he knew he needed help but did not know where to turn. He had the business card of a pastor friend, so he called him, and the pastor said, "Come on up here. I'll provide a place for you to stay, and you can help around the church. We're going to pray and believe God for your deliverance."

One day as my friend was praying, the Lord spoke to him and told him he was going to go to Brazil! My friend said, "Lord, I don't even know anybody in Brazil."

That very night in church, a missionary from Brazil spoke to the congregation! While he was there, the missionary asked the pastor and my friend to go back to Brazil with him! My friend said, "Well, I really would like to go, but I don't have the money."

The pastor said, "We'll take care of everything." So the pastor and my friend arranged to fly to Brazil.

The two got off the airplane in Brazil, put their luggage in a hotel, and went straight to a meeting. At the meeting, they were immediately invited to sit on the platform. My friend was sitting next to a certain Brazilian pastor. This pastor kept looking at my friend, patting him on the leg and weeping. Now this Brazilian pastor had lost one leg. He just had one leg and part of another one. My friend could not understand why he was weeping.

After the service, the Brazilian pastor introduced himself and invited the pastor and my friend to preach at his church. It was an old airplane hangar way out in the countryside that they had converted to a church. My friend's pastor preached, and, after the service, the Brazilian pastor asked my friend to stay another week to pray with him. My friend said to me later, "I don't even know why I did it, but I just felt like I should stay, so I agreed."

Well, the only place to stay was in the back of the church where there were two cots. That is where the pastor lived. They could not speak each other's language, but they were together for a week.

During the middle of the night on the first night — about three o'clock in the morning — this Brazilian pastor woke up my friend and said, "Pray! Pray! Pray!"

So they got out of bed, went into the church, prayed for about an hour, and went back to bed.

The next night, the Brazilian pastor did the same thing. They got up and prayed and went back to bed.

This happened every night. Finally, on the last night, my friend had said to himself, *If he wakes me up again tonight, I'm not getting up!*

Sure enough, at three o'clock in the morning, the Brazilian pastor woke him up, saying, "Pray! Pray! Pray!" My friend said, "Well, this is the last night, so I'll go ahead and pray with the man."

In the church, the Brazilian pastor was just praying away. My friend said he was just half-heartedly praying. He told me, "As we were praying, all of a sudden, the top of the building just 'opened up.' A light out of Heaven came shining down through the roof of that building."

My friend said that the light 'hit' him in the top of the head and went all the way through him, all the way down through his toes. And it totally purged all of the uncleanness out of him. It completely cleansed him! He said, "It was like I was a pure, clean, new person. I could not even believe that I was the person who had done all the junk that I did."

The next morning after that experience, the interpreters were present, so my friend said to the Brazilian pastor, "Please tell me what you know. I know you didn't just wake me up every night for no reason."

The Brazilian pastor told him, "Twenty years ago I was praying, and I saw your face." (Twenty years before that time, my friend hadn't even been *saved* yet, much less in the ministry and then backslidden!)

The Brazilian pastor continued, "I saw your face in a vision twenty years ago. Then five years ago, it was discovered that I had cancer. Doctors told me I was going to die, but I said 'God, I cannot die, because I have not seen this American, and You told me that I was going to help bring his deliverance.'" God healed this pastor of the cancer.

So you can understand why this Brazilian man was weeping and crying when he first saw my friend. Twenty years before that time, God had already prepared a way! God knew from the beginning of time that my friend was going to serve Him and that he was going to fall into sin. So He prepared a way of deliverance for him, and He found a man down in Brazil at a little ol' country church. Then He brought my friend to Brazil and got him delivered!

Now my friend did die of cancer a couple of years later, but he is in Heaven. He had been gloriously delivered. God went before him and provided a way!

God Has Prepared Your Way

There is no trial or adversity that you are facing for which God has not already prepared a way out. It is there. All you have to do is obey Him, and God will bring it about in your life.

In my own life, I think about the time Becky and I were separated fourteen months. Neither of us had any desire to get back together. We were not living for God; we were going our own way. Yet God had already made a way of deliverance for us. He supernaturally got us back together. He guided us back to Houston, Texas, and placed us where we could hear the Word of God and receive Jesus and all the fullness of God. Then He called us to the ministry. God has a way!

What I'm telling you is very important, because God has made a way for your deliverance too. He has gone before you to prepare a way. You can sit there and whine and cry if you want to, saying, "There's no way. There's just no way for me." God *has* made a way! He has gone before you.

There is a way. God has a place. There is a divine destiny for your deliverance. It doesn't matter whether it is financial, physical, mental — whatever it is — God has provided the way. He has gone before you to provide it. Maybe the way is in a place out there that you do not even know about today. Just keep following the Lord. Maybe it is in a person whom you do not know today. Or maybe it is not in a person; it could be just a situation or circumstance. I don't know, but I know God has gone before you to provide it. Just don't give up or give in. Keep on believing and expecting. It will come.

If you would have talked to my friend who had gone into such darkness, at one point, he would have probably told you, "There is no hope." He was in his pastor friend's church, but he was still struggling over the darkness inside him because of everything he had done. God had already made a way for him. Twenty years prior to my friend's being bound up, God had gone before him and made a way!

Be encouraged! God has done the same for you. He has gone before you and has made a way. Just keep walking with Him and following Him, and He will show you the way out. Your situation is not impossible. There is no bondage you can get into in which you can say, "It's impossible" if you really want to be free.

I know a man who was "destined" for prison. He was given a twenty-year sentence for attempted murder. The authorities had the gun with his fingerprints on it. This man got saved, filled with the Holy Ghost, and was called to the ministry. Then he went to trial. He told the Lord, "I know You've called me, but I'm going to prison." He thought he was going to have a prison ministry.

During the trial, his attorney said, "We want those fingerprints examined again." When the prints were reexamined, they didn't match! They weren't his fingerprints! You talk about God making a way where there does not seem to be a way! (I'm not saying this situation will always be God's plan in every similar case. But I am saying that, with God, there is a way to be loosed from the taskmaster!)

Let me say something else about God's making a way for your deliverance. Oftentimes, people think that the way the Lord is making *toward* their deliverance actually *is* their deliverance! That is not always the case. For example, someone may be struggling financially. God provides a way for him to pay his rent, and he says, "Oh, thank God! I'm delivered!" But, no, he just got his rent paid. Unless he comes out of that situation of struggling financially and living "hand-to-mouth," he is still in bondage to the taskmaster financially.

What is God doing when He makes certain provision, such as a rent payment? He is just making a way to get you to the place He wants you to be. Do not stop there. He wants to deliver you all the way!

If you get delivered all the way, you will never want to go back to "Egypt." People who want to go back into the world never made it into their promised land. They are still wandering around in the wilderness, so to speak. They are still struggling. The children of Israel who wandered around in the wilderness for forty years were always looking back to Egypt.

So do not settle for the wilderness. God wants to bring you out of bondage to a place of abundance — a place of complete deliverance!

Freedom Principle Number Nine:
Don't Become Discouraged
When You Reach an Impasse

The ninth freedom principle you need to know to obtain your deliverance is found in refusing to be discouraged and expecting to see the glory of God every time you run into trouble. The neglect of this principle keeps more people in trouble than you can imagine.

The Old Testament says that when the children of Israel were led out of the land of Egypt, they were greatly blessed. There was not a sick person among the children of Israel. They had the Egyptians' silver and gold. The Bible says, "God delivered them with a *high* hand" (Exod. 14:8)! God had the original "high-five"! Then Pharaoh changed his mind, and the Egyptians started pursuing God's people across the Red Sea. Once again, God wrought a mighty deliverance.

Let us review what happened in the great deliverance God wrought when the Egyptians were pursuing God's people.

EXODUS 14:9-12
**9 But the Egyptians pursued after them, all the horses
and chariots of Pharaoh, and his horsemen, and his army,
and overtook them encamping by the sea, beside Pihahi-
roth, before Baalzephon.**
**10 And when Pharaoh drew nigh, the children of Israel
lifted up their eyes, and, behold, the Egyptians marched
after them; and they were sore afraid: and the children of
Israel cried out unto the Lord.**
**11 And they said unto Moses, Because there were no
graves in Egypt, hast thou taken us away to die in the
wilderness? wherefore hast thou dealt thus with us, to
carry us forth out of Egypt?**
**12 Is not this the word that we did tell thee in Egypt, say-
ing, Let us alone, that we may serve the Egyptians? For it
had been better for us to serve the Egyptians, than that
we should die in the wilderness.**

Notice what the children of Israel said when the Egyptian armies pursued them. God had already led them out of
Egypt, but they ran into some trouble at the Red Sea, so
they began murmuring and complaining, saying to Moses,
"It would have been better for us to serve the Egyptians! It
would have been better to have avoided this whole mess!"

Once God has delivered you, you have to be careful
what you say when you run into trouble. I have had Christians tell me, "I was better off in the world." They are just
like this bunch in Exodus 14!

Notice that Moses paid no attention to them.

EXODUS 14:13,14
**13 And Moses said unto the people, Fear ye not, stand still,
and see the salvation of the Lord, which he will shew to you
to day: for the Egyptians whom ye have seen to day, ye shall
see them again no more for ever.**
**14 The Lord shall fight for you, and ye shall hold your
peace.**

In other words, Moses told them, "Shut up! God will take care of this just as He has taken care of everything else!"

Here is what I want you to see. If you are going to receive God's deliverance, do not allow yourself to become discouraged when you reach an impasse — a place where it looks like the end for you or as if it is all over.

Someone might say, "Well, I thought God was going to deliver me. It looked like He was. I've seen supernatural signs, and I've been following God, but, dear God, look at me now! The situation looks worse than ever!"

Have you ever been there? I have. I know the feeling. However, I have enough experience now to just look at those situations, smile, and say, "Well, there is a way out of this. God is making a way."

If you want to receive deliverance, you must not be discouraged when it looks like there is no way out.

I want to ask you a question. Had God already seen that impasse at the Red Sea when the Egyptians were bearing down on the children of Israel? Yes, He had, and because He had already seen it, He had also prepared a way out. He made a path through the mighty waters.

> **ISAIAH 43:16**
> **16 Thus saith the Lord, which maketh a way in the sea, and a path in the mighty waters.**

God is the God who makes a way through the sea — through the mighty waters! And He made a supernatural way for the children of Israel through the middle of the sea! God knew what was going to happen, and He had already spelled it out. He saw that path through the waters. He knew what He was going to do. The Israelites didn't know it, but God did. That is why they needed to look to Him and just trust Him.

Your Impasse Could Be Your Deliverance!

You see, many times, your impasse is the very way of your deliverance! That was the case with the children of Israel at the Red Sea. With the Egyptians on one side and the Red Sea on the other, the Red Sea became the avenue of their deliverance. So the very thing you think is going to be your "downfall" could be your deliverance!

God knows how to deliver you. So do not become discouraged when there is an impasse. Just start looking for the path through the waters! Don't ask, "God, where are You going to part the Red Sea? How are You going to do this?" Quit all of that senseless talk about, "We would have been better off if we had never even started this. We're just going to go back over to the First Church!"

Now don't get upset with me if you have ever said anything like that. I am just telling you the truth. Actually, this is a common attitude that many Christians have today. They want to go back into "Egypt." They want to go back to the old way.

I always ask, "Well, if the old way was so good, why didn't you just stay there? Why did you want to be delivered in the first place!"

Some will say, "Well, I wanted to be delivered because there wasn't anything there for me."

I ask, "Then what would you be going back to?"

You see, the children of Israel were constantly dreaming about the garlic and leeks of Egypt that they ate. I do not think that tasted very good at all! It probably *wasn't* very good, but because they were now in the wilderness eating manna every day, they just *imagined* that garlic and leeks were good!

We know that God will make a way through the waters. So do not become discouraged, saying, "Oh, dear God, this is it. It's over now." No, it's not over until God moves on your behalf, and you win!

Be Careful What You Say!

So when it seems as if you have come to an impasse in life, be careful what you say. Do not start confessing what you do not want! God had mercy on the children of Israel when they said, "We were better off in Egypt...yackety yack yack..."! However, they pulled that stunt again in Numbers 12 when they were standing at the Jordan River, and God held them to their words. They said, "We can't go there because of all the giants in the land. We should have died in the wilderness!" God had put up with their grumbling long enough, and He said, "All right, you've got it. That is exactly what you're going to do — you are going to die in the wilderness."

That is why it is so important to watch what you say. When there is seemingly an impasse in your life, do not start talking about things you do not really want. If you do, those things may not happen the first or second time you say it; however, if you say it enough, you will start getting what you say. Then you will wonder why God "forsook" you. He did not forsake you; you just used your own mouth to stop your deliverance!

So keep a watch over your tongue! Moses basically told the children of Israel, "Hold your peace. Just be quiet."

I am convinced that if we would just keep our mouths shut, God could do more for us. So when things look bad, put your hand over your mouth if you have to! Why? Because God may want to do something! That is exactly what happened at the Red Sea. Moses said, "Fear not! Stand still and see the salvation of the Lord!"

Many times, people get too "antsy." They become impatient, and they start saying, "What am I going to do? I must have missed a turn somewhere. There's no deliverance here. What am I going to do now? How am I going to fix this?" What they need to do is just stand still!

Someone said, "Yes, Pastor Carr, but you just don't understand. There's no way out of this!"

Yes, there is a way! You just don't see it. So just stand still.

"Well, what's going to happen if I stand still?" You are going to see the deliverance of the Lord, because the Lord is going to fight for you!

You see, all you have to do is give Him the opportunity. It is not as if you have to talk Him into helping you! He loves you. He wants to work in your life. He wants to lift you up. He wants to guide you. He wants to bring you into your promised land!

God wants to bring liberty in your life and break every yoke of the taskmaster! He wants to heal your body and deliver your soul! "Pastor Carr, how do you know that?" Jesus said so in Luke 4:18.

LUKE 4:18
18 The Spirit of the Lord is upon me, because he hath anointed me to preach the gospel to the poor; he hath sent me to heal the brokenhearted, to preach deliverance to the captives, and

recovering of sight to the blind, to set at liberty them that are bruised.

So when you reach an impasse in life, just stop. Stand still. Keep your mouth shut. That is hard to do, because human nature wants to do something to fix the situation. I have had people tell me, "I've been believing God, and now my situation is worse. What did I do wrong?"

I ask, "Did you ever stop to think you may be doing something right?"

"Well, yes, but everything looks wrong."

When a situation looks bad, that does not mean it is going to be bad. Think about the children of Israel at the Red Sea. There was seemingly no way out. If you were there, you might have said, "Something is wrong here. We missed a turn on the freeway somewhere. We're going in the wrong direction, because there is no way out of this." God had not misled the children of Israel. They were going in the right direction all along.

So, as I said, learn to watch what you say. Learn to be still before the Lord and wait on Him. Let Him work. When you do, you will see the supernatural deliverance of the Lord!

Freedom Principle Number Ten:
Make Sure the Taskmaster Is Dead!

Let us continue reading in Exodus 14 concerning freedom principle number ten.

EXODUS 14:26-28
26 And the Lord said unto Moses, Stretch out thine hand over the sea, that the waters may come again upon the Egyptians, upon their chariots, and upon their horsemen.

27 And Moses stretched forth his hand over the sea, and the sea returned to his strength when the morning appeared; and the Egyptians fled against it; and the Lord overthrew the Egyptians in the midst of the sea.
28 And the waters returned, and covered the chariots, and the horsemen, and all host of Pharaoh that came into the sea after them; there remained not so much as one of them.

I like verse 28. When God led the children of Israel across the sea on dry land, *"...the waters returned, and covered the chariots, and the horsemen, and all the host of Pharaoh that came into the sea after them; there remained not so much as one of them."* All the Egyptian soldiers were dead!

Always remember, you are not out of "Egypt" until the taskmaster is dead. You have to kill that dude! You cannot just wound him and hope he doesn't bother you anymore. You can't just say, "Well, I can live with that. I can get by."

In other words, whatever that thing is that has kept you in bondage, you need to know that it is dead — that it is over with and that it has no more power or authority over you. So freedom principle number ten is, make sure the taskmaster you have been freed from is dead. Kill it. Make sure it has no more influence on your life. Make sure that it is gone forever.

The Bible says in Exodus 14:27 that "the Egyptians fled against it," referring to the sea which had returned to its strength after the Israelites crossed over. Then it says, *"...and the Lord overthrew the Egyptians in the midst of the sea."*

That word "overthrew" in this verse means *to shake off.* It means that God literally shook off the Egyptians.

There may be some things holding you in bondage, but God wants you to shake them off! He wants you to be free of them. He does not want them to control you anymore or to ever return. He wants them dead so that they cannot haunt and torment you anymore.

You are going to have to make up your mind, "Bless God, I am going to throw this off! I'm going to get rid of it! I'm not going to be under the control of this anymore. God is going to deliver me!"

The Bible says, "There remained not so much as one of them," referring to the Egyptian soldiers. Not one of the pursuing Egyptian army or the pursuing problem was left to confront God's people!

I do not want to be critical of anything in the natural that helps people. For example, I know of a program that has delivered many people, especially in the area of alcohol. They go through a "step" program. On that last step, they had better kill that devil, or it will come back to haunt them!

You had better know that the taskmaster is dead in your life. You need to shake him off and know that it is over. You need to be able to say, "I'm going forward with my life. I'm delivered in Jesus' Name."

When God brings deliverance in your life, you have the ability to "shake it off." You can make sure that whatever it was that bound you has no more authority or control over your life.

Now I am not talking as a novice. I have sat in some of those kinds of meetings. I have seen many those people come and go. The reason they leave is, they do get some deliverance. However, they did not kill that devil in their life. They did not kill the taskmaster that enslaved them to drink. They did not shake it off. He was still around.

"How do you know all that?" you might ask. I have seen it happen over and over again. I saw it happen in my own father's life. My dad was an alcoholic. He drank all the time, and I am not talking about just a little bit of alcohol. He would drink a fifth of vodka like you or I would drink water! He did it every day, day in and day out.

But when my father made Jesus the Lord of his life at the age of sixty, instantly, he shook it off. He shook off the taskmaster of alcoholism. Its power was broken in his life. The yoke was broken, and he did not have to be concerned about, "Well, what if I drink again?" No, it was gone. He had drunk all of his life, but God delivered him!

Shake Off the Taskmaster Completely!

It does not matter what taskmaster it is that has bound you, do not just get enough deliverance so that you are feeling better and everything is "fine." No, shake it off *completely*! Make sure that it has no power over you. The only way that is going to happen is if you do it supernaturally.

You see, the children of Israel walked on dry ground across that sea supernaturally. It was a supernatural deliverance. That is what God wants to do for you. You just need to stay on top of the situation every day. Just stomp on that taskmaster every day and say, "No, you're not coming back. You're dead. You're not controlling my life any longer."

Freedom Principle Number Eleven:
Take No Counsel From the World —
Your Deliverance Is the World's Downfall

Let's look again at Exodus chapter 14.

EXODUS 14:22-25
22 And the children of Israel went into the midst of the sea upon the dry ground: and the waters were a wall unto them on their right hand, and on their left.
23 And the Egyptians pursued, and went in after them to the midst of the sea, even all Pharaoh's horses, his chariots, and his horsemen.
24 And it came to pass, that in the morning watch the Lord looked unto the host of the Egyptians through the pillar of fire and of the cloud, and troubled the host of the Egyptians,
25 And took off their chariot wheels, that they drave them heavily: so that the Egyptians said, Let us flee from the face of Israel; for the Lord fighteth for them against the Egyptians.

Look at the last part of verse 25. The Egyptians had already experienced God's judgments in the form of the flies, the frogs, the blood, the pestilence, and the slayings of the first-born children of the Egyptians. Finally, in the middle of the Red Sea, the Egyptians figured it out: "*...the Lord fighteth for them...*"! It finally occurred to them that the Lord was working with the children of Israel!

Keep on reading in verses 26 and 27 to see an interesting difference between the believer and the world.

EXODUS 14:26,27
26 And the Lord said unto Moses, Stretch out thine hand over the sea, that the waters may come again upon the Egyptians, upon their chariots, and upon their horsemen.
27 And Moses stretched forth his hand over the sea, and the

sea returned to his strength when the morning appeared; and the Egyptians fled against it; and the Lord overthrew the Egyptians in the midst of the sea.

In these verses, we can see that Israel's deliverance was Egypt's downfall, just as your deliverance is the world's downfall. What is deliverance to the believer will trip up the world. Your deliverance comes from God, not from the world system. Therefore, whatever you do to cooperate with and obey God for your deliverance is going be different from the world.

For example, the world says concerning finances, "You need to invest and you need to save. You need to protect your money. You need to be careful about your finances." In and of itself, that advice is not bad, but if you walk strictly in the world's counsel, you will not be blessed, because the Bible says to *give*, and it shall be given unto you. God's way of getting money to you is through your *giving*. You will not get that kind of counsel from the world. The Bible also says, *"He that hath pity upon the poor lendeth unto the Lord; and that which he hath given will he pay him again"* (Prov. 19:17).

Your way of deliverance is not the way of the world. The Bible says to give out, not to hoard and hold back, your money. Now the world may even try what you do, but it will not work for them. They will lose everything they have. Why? It may look the same, but it is not the same. What God tells you to do is a supernatural avenue of deliverance for you! However, without God, just doing certain things and going through the motions, so to speak, does not work. It does not bring about a supernatural result.

I will give you an example of this from the Word of God. It is the story of the seven sons of Sceva. The Book of Acts tells the story. Paul and others had been casting out devils in the Name of Jesus. And so these seven men said, "Well, if they can do it, we can use the Name too."

Yet when they tried it, the devils said, *"Jesus* we know, and *Paul* we know, but who are *you*?" Then the devils jumped on them, stripped off their garments, and beat them up! And the seven men fled, naked (*see* Acts 19:13-16).

On the one hand, the Name of Jesus brought deliverance. On the other hand, it brought destruction.

You see, the world cannot use our system of deliverance. Don't ever let the world con you into believing that your way — God's way — is wrong. I read a newspaper article recently that reported a scientific finding that laughter can make you healthy! The world discovered that, but the Bible has said that for years! Christians have known that was true since the time the Bible was written!

So the world has "discovered" this, but don't you think for one minute that they will use this avenue of deliverance the way many Christians use it. For example, if some people from the world walked in to one of my church services in which the joy of the Lord was "hitting," they would say, "Those people are crazy!" They would not realize that it was our deliverance!

The world does not know deliverance when they see it. The world says, "You have to protect yourself, you know. You have to be careful. You don't want to talk to strangers, and you have to be careful about your surroundings." However, the Bible says, "Just walk in love." For us, love works, because we are children of God. The world could try to walk in love, but it would not work. They cannot operate in the same kind of love we operate in. It has to be the God-kind of love, and there has to be a godly motive.

With the world, their benevolence usually has some sort of hidden motive — a "hitch" or "catch." Most corporate sponsors of certain charitable events, for example, don't support those events because the love of God dwells in them. They do it because they will get publicity; they will get their company name before the public. Yet in the Church, there are people ministering and reaching out to others every day, yet the public never knows their names.

That is what I mean when I say our deliverance is the world's downfall. The world cannot do what you do. They might try to "impersonate" you, but they cannot.

Recently, in America, a great secular campaign has begun regarding volunteerism. Well, that is the world's counterfeit for servantship.

You see, we, the Body of Christ, are servants. That is what works. True servantship is only going to work through the Church. That is where the spirit of servantship is. The people who have gone before us who have truly served were a part of the Church. It is not being in authority that gets the job done. The government has been trying to say that it can do what the Church has done. They imply, "We don't need the Church to serve and to build great universities and hospitals. We can do it. We can have volunteers, and it will be the same." The way the world does things is *not* the same! We Christians live a different kind of life. It brings deliverance to us and to others, but when the world tries to do the same, it does not bring godly deliverance.

The trap the Church has fallen into is that we have let the world tell us what is right and wrong and what is good and bad. We have allowed the Church to be exploited. If we will just go God's way instead of the world's way and obey the Word of God, real deliverance will come to us. We do not have to go by what the world system says.

For example, if you need a financial miracle in your life, you should just obey what God says. You do it God's way and stay with it. You don't call "A-1 Finance Company" and let them consolidate your bills, thinking that's going to get you out of debt. Many people do that and then get right back into debt again. Then not only do they have the finance company to pay, but they have all those credit-card companies to pay too!

God has a better way for you. His way is never the world's way. So you might as well make up your mind you are going do it God's way, because the world's way goes up and down, in and out, and round about! It's always changing, but God's way never changes. It is always available. It is always sound. It always brings deliverance to your life.

Now, many times, the world will think you are crazy for following God. They do not understand spiritual things. Therefore, they will not understand the way you are operating. They will not understand what the Spirit of God is doing in our church services, setting people free supernaturally. Yet it brings deliverance to the people of God.

Remember God parted the Red Sea for His people to cross over on dry land. How did God do that? Basically, He made "gelatin" of the sea, and it brought deliverance to His people! It was not the world's deliverance; it was God's deliverance. It worked for the children of Israel, but when the world, the Egyptians, tried it, it was their downfall.

Theologians have tried to explain away the deliverance at the Red Sea by saying things, such as, "Well, you know, it wasn't a big sea at that time. Actually, it was just a small creek, about two-feet deep, that they passed over."

Well, if that was the case, it was an even bigger miracle, because an entire army of Egyptians was drowned in two feet of water!

So take no counsel from the world, because your deliverance is the world's downfall. Do not become double-minded, trying to live life both God's way and the world's way. Just stay with God's way, and God will bring real, supernatural deliverance to you.

Let us review the eleven freedom principles I have shared from the Word of God.

1. **Receive a revelation of your new beginning.**
2. **Be obedient to the terms of the sacrifice.**
3. **Be prepared for change.**
4. **Expect a supernatural sign.**
5. **Put spiritual things first.**
6. **Worship God for your deliverance.**
7. **Be ready to receive.**
8. **Know that God will go before you and make a way!**
9. **Don't become discouraged when you reach an impasse.**

10. **Make sure the taskmaster is dead!**
11. **Take no counsel from the world — your deliverance is the world's downfall.**

God doesn't just want to deliver you; He wants to bring you into your promised land, into a place of abundance. Whatever bondage you find yourself in, remember that God wants you to be free. And you can be free. You can be loosed from the taskmaster!

How To Build A Better Life.

~~How~~

1. Enter Into A Relationship
With God.   a. The plan of God.
             b. He wants you!
             c. How to the Spirit
2. Understand how God views
   you as a person.
3. understand your rights &
   priviledges as a Christian
4. Receive the baptism of
   the Holy Spirit Go on a missions trips
5. Develop an attitude of
   gratitude.
6. ~~Become~~ Learn how to ~~work~~
   ~~with people~~ love all types of people.
7. Become a giver not a giver.
   a. Friendship
8. Learn how to manage your
   time & money.
9. ~~Read~~ Make the Bible your
   number one book.
10. Develop a strong prayer life
11. Know what your purpose in
    life is & God's.
12. Put your best behind
    you and build toward the future.
    a. Search for employment